W9-BRA-499

For the Birds

PAPER-PIECED
BIRDHOUSES AND BIRD FEEDERS

JAYNETTE HUFF

Martingale
& COMPANY™

For the Birds: Paper-Pieced Birdhouses and Bird Feeders
© 2001 by Jaynette Huff

Martingale & Company
PO Box 118
Bothell, WA 98041-0118
www.martingale-pub.com

Credits

President: Nancy J. Martin
CEO: Daniel J. Martin
Publisher: Jane Hamada
Editorial Director: Mary V. Green
Editorial Project Manager: Tina Cook
Technical Editor: Laurie Baker
Copy Editor: Pamela Mostek
Design and Production Manager: Stan Green
Illustrator: Robin Strobel
Cover and Text Designer: Rohani Design
Photographer: Brent Kane

Printed in China
06 05 04 03 02   8 7 6 5 4 3 2

Library of Congress Cataloging-in-Publication Data

Huff, Jaynette.
   For the birds : paper-pieced patterns of bird houses and
   bird feeders / Jaynette Huff.
      p. cm.
   ISBN 1-56477-365-5
   1. Patchwork—Patterns. 2. Patchwork quilts.
   3. Birdhouses in art. 4. Bird feeders in art. I. Title.

TT835 .H7897 2001
746.46'041—dc21   2001030865

Dedication

To my husband Larry. Thank you for your love and support. You truly are a joy. And to the mothers and grandmothers in my life who all have had an appreciation for the beauty of birds in their backyards and farmlands: Ida Mae Borders, Velma C. Parker, Etta Huff, Betty Hineline, and Aleta Borders. Although none were official "birdwatchers," they all expressed an admiration for the grace, the colors, and the music of bird songs.

Acknowledgments

To Julia Dascanio, who paper-pieced many of the blocks used in the quilts presented in this book. Her workmanship was well done and allowed me the time to concentrate on the block settings and the written portions of this book.

To Judie Kline, who paper-pieced the blocks for "Birds' Picnic in the Park," but even more, who offered careful critique and suggestions when I was selecting border fabrics and colors. I appreciate your sense of color, your thoughtful comments, and your "artist's eye."

To Valerie Schraml, who once again took on the job of converting my writing to the correct manuscript format. Thank you.

To the Husqvarna Viking Sewing Machine Company for the loan of a Designer I sewing/embroidery machine. I thoroughly enjoyed adding the dimension of fine machine embroidery to "At Home in the Rose Garden."

To Laurie Baker, who served once more as the technical editor for my book. I loved what she did for the first book and knew I could rely on her suggestions to improve the second.

To Martingale & Company, especially Mary Green and Dawn Anderson, who once more allowed me to present my ideas and designs in a book format. It has been a joy to work for and with the people of Martingale. Their acceptance and encouragement of my work provides great motivation and pride.

To the women who work at Idle-Hour Quilts and Design. Your interest and encouragement are greatly appreciated.

And especially to all those quilters who participated in the original "For the Birds Block-of-the-Month" program offered through my shop. I can hardly wait to see the wall hangings and quilts that result from your efforts. Thank you for your involvement!

Contents

INTRODUCTION 4

PREPARING TO BUILD 5

Tools and Supplies 5

Fabric Selection and Preparation 6

Construction Terminology 8

BUILDING BIRDHOUSES AND FEEDERS 9

Steps to Successful Paper
Foundation Piecing 9

Framing Your Projects 15

Fine Finishes 19

BASIC HANGING BIRDHOUSE 25

BUNGALOW BIRDHOUSE 27

RUSTIC CABIN BIRDHOUSE 29

SCHOOLHOUSE BIRDHOUSE 31

SECOND EMPIRE-STYLE BIRDHOUSE 33

TURRET BIRDHOUSE 35

WOVEN BASKET BIRDHOUSE 37

BOTTLE BIRD FEEDER 39

COACH LANTERN BIRD FEEDER 41

COVERED TRAY BIRD FEEDER 43

DOUBLE-SIDED ARBOR BIRD FEEDER 45

HUMMINGBIRD FEEDER 47

SHED ROOF BIRD FEEDER 49

BUTTERFLY HOUSE 51

FINCH FEEDER 54

POLE BIRDHOUSE 57

TWO-STORY BIRDHOUSE 60

BLOSSOMS 64

BLUEBIRD 66

CHICKADEE 67

DOVE 68

BRANCH 69

INDIVIDUAL-BLOCK WALL HANGINGS 72

ALL AROUND THE NEIGHBORHOOD 74

AT HOME IN THE ROSE GARDEN 78

FLY AWAY HOME 84

HOME FOR THE HOLIDAYS 87

IT'S A BIRDS' PICNIC IN THE PARK 90

SPRINGTIME DELIGHT 93

ABOUT THE AUTHOR 96

introduction

Today we are seeing many people enjoying building and decorating birdhouses—not only for the birds in their backyards but also to decorate the inside of their homes. Perhaps this is to create a peaceful vignette or mental sanctuary, a momentary rest or refuge where they can meditate, dream, clear their minds of worry, and achieve a feeling of tranquility and peace. I have just such a birdhouse vignette on my fireplace mantle. It is a large wooden birdhouse in the shape of a country church with a tall steeple. It sits on a small quilt that hangs

down over the mantle and has a green plant placed beside it. When I look at it, it brings a sense of peace into my mind, an escape from the TV, the phone, and day-to-day worries.

One has only to look in the libraries and bookstores at the large number of books written on the subject to realize how popular building birdhouses and feeders has become. This book, too, deals with building birdhouses and bird feeders, but it has been designed for sewers and quilters. A wide variety of designs has been included, from the simple basic hanging birdhouse to the more complicated two-story structure. The pattern collection includes seven birdhouses (each 7" x 9"); six bird feeders (each 7" x 9"); four long, tall houses and/or feeders (each 7" x 18"); five smaller companion blocks (each 4" x 4"); and one long, leafy branch (4½" x 34"). Use a single block pattern to create a small wall hanging or combine several patterns to create a variety of quilt sizes and arrangements to suit your taste or preference. A total of seven different block settings or quilt arrangements has been provided.

We start the building process with a listing and explanation of building materials, tools, and equipment in the section entitled "Tools and Supplies." Any building project you take on is bound to involve tools and special equipment. Not just any tool, but the right tool correctly used. This means learning all that you can about the sewing tools and their purposes and mastering the technique that each one requires. It is precisely this kind of instruction, applied to the building of these quilted birdhouses and feeders, that you will find in this section. As with any construction, your ability and experience, as well as the quality of your tools and supplies, makes a significant difference. Choose to use the best you can afford.

The terminology used for building these birdhouses and feeders is defined and discussed in the section entitled "Construction Terminology" (page 8), while a discussion of fabric selection is included in "Fabric Selection and Preparation" (page 6).

In addition to supplying information so you can prepare to build, this book serves as a builder's guide to the steps in constructing the houses and feeders. The section entitled "Building Birdhouses and Feeders" (pages 9–24) provides such instruction. Be sure to consult the tables and diagrams that accompany the text in the various sections. They are provided to help you understand the steps more quickly and to take the correct building/sewing action.

A detailed explanation of how to effectively frame your blocks with accurate $\frac{1}{4}$" borders is provided in "Framing Your Projects" (pages 15–18). Careful attention to these steps and diagrams can help to create truly stunning block settings.

Of course, the basic structure is not the end of the story. Instructions for finishing touches are given in the section entitled "Fine Finishes" (pages 19–24) so you can bring out the personality of your birdhouse. Topics include embellishments, embroidery, quilting, and binding.

Periodically there are small boxed areas that provide more detailed directions and information about related topics, such as mitered corners or basic color principles. These are to provide useful hints for better building of your projects.

Let these birdhouse and bird feeder designs spark your imagination. Create a natural color habitat using browns and greens, or let your imagination create whimsical and glorious structures from bright colors. Wild and crazy has a place here too. The point is that you have the ability, the materials, and the supplies, and with this book, the "know-how," to create your own mental sanctuary, your own "moment of beauty," the retreat you need to cope more effectively with the busyness of your life. I wish you years of pleasure in whatever kind of bird sanctuary you build.

Get out there and sew something beautiful—for the birds!

Preparing to Build

TOOLS AND SUPPLIES

Just like the builder who constructs wooden birdhouses, you will need special tools and supplies to make it easier to paper piece fabric birdhouses. The items listed and briefly discussed below will be very useful to include in your own sewing "tool box."

- All-purpose thread for machine piecing blocks and borders. Choose only good quality, 100 percent–cotton thread. A neutral tan or gray works well with most fabrics.

- Batting. There are many kinds of batting available. Choose the one that gives you the desired result.
- Beading needle for attaching embellishments
- Beads for embellishing blocks
- Buttons to serve as "entry holes" and "perches." Choose a variety of sizes and colors to enhance each house or feeder.
- Colored markers for making reference marks on your foundation paper. I recommend fine-line markers in four to five different colors.

- Darning foot or open-toe appliqué foot for free-motion machine quilting
- Design wall, which is optional, but you will find it helpful when deciding overall block placement
- Embroidery floss for block embellishment and outlining details
- Even-feed foot or walking foot for straight-line machine quilting
- Fabric markers to draw the extended seam lines on the wrong side of the fabric for the ¼" borders. Depending on the fabric color, you may need one for dark fabrics and one for light fabrics.
- Freezer paper, the recommended paper for the foundation pattern (commercially available)
- Iron and ironing board that is set up within easy reach, as you will use it following every fabric addition. An iron with a steam setting is preferred.
- Light box. This handy tool makes it easier to trace the pattern onto freezer paper, as well as to transfer embellishment placement lines onto the pieced unit. You may also use a window or create your own (page 10).
- Machine quilting thread such as YLI nylon monofilament, which I recommend. Use clear for light fabrics and smoke for dark fabrics.
- Mechanical pencil for tracing the pattern onto freezer paper foundation
- Pins to secure the parts together when matching pieces and later for sashing and border attachment. I recommend extra-long, glass-head silk pins.
- Quilting needle, hand or machine (quilter's preference)
- Rotary cutter, cutting mat, and rulers. Select a mat no smaller than 17" x 23" and a small- or medium-size cutter. A 6" x 24" ruler with ¼" marks is necessary for cutting strips. For trimming pattern parts, you will need a smaller ruler (6" x 6"or 4" x 8"). If desired, purchase a 12½" x 12½" ruler for squaring-up your work.
- Safety pins for possible pin-basting. Use rustproof safety pins in a size 0 or 1 only.
- Scissors of a good quality that you are willing to use for cutting both paper and fabric. Smaller 5" embroidery size works especially well for easy pickup and trimming. Thread clippers are also helpful.
- Seam ripper (optional, but a good idea)
- Sewing machine in good working condition. A simple straight-stitch machine with reverse capability is all that is required. The recommended stitch length is fifteen to twenty stitches per inch.
- Sewing machine needles. I recommend a size 80/12 or 90/14 for paper foundation piecing.
- Stiletto, a sharp pointed instrument that helps separate stubbornly adhered paper and fabric pieces
- Trash bag for trimmings
- Tweezers for removing the paper foundation in tiny, hard-to-reach corners and crevices

FABRIC SELECTION AND PREPARATION

A good craftsman takes the time to carefully look over the materials available, whether selecting wood, paint, trim—or fabric. Keep the following guidelines in mind as you select the fabrics to use in your projects.

- Use only top quality, 100 percent–cotton fabrics. Don't waste your time and energy trying to make poor quality fabrics work for you.
- Provide contrast in value, scale, and intensity. All three can add interest, variety, and life to your work (see "Basic Color Principles" on page 7).
- Look for a variety of tone-on-tone prints, tiny all-over prints, and coordinating companion fabrics. These types of prints tend to work well in these blocks and with this technique. They provide visual interest, texture, and design, but they do not detract from the shape of the structures themselves.
- Approach directional prints and large-scale prints with caution. Directional prints can lead to added frustration as you attempt to make them "go in the right direction." And large-scale prints, bold geometrics, or busy stripes and plaids may actually overpower the design of the structures and confuse the viewer. Save these types of prints for sashings and borders.

BASIC COLOR PRINCIPLES

Value. Value is the difference between the lightness and darkness of fabric colors. Within your quilt you need to incorporate fabrics of light, medium, and dark values. Of course, value is a relative term. The fabric of darkest value in one quilt may be of only medium value in another.

Scale. Variety in fabric scale adds interest to a quilt. Scale refers to the size of the designs printed on the fabrics. When choosing your fabrics, select large-, medium-, and small-size prints. Of course, scale like value is relative. What is considered small in one quilt may be medium in another. Further, what is appropriate scale will vary with factors such as block design and piecing technique. Due to the small block size in these patterns, large-scale prints are probably inappropriate for the blocks but not for the borders.

Intensity. How brilliant or intense are the colors of the fabrics chosen? A little bit of bright or strong intensity can go a long way, but its absence can bury your quilt in dullness and boredom. A touch of color intensity can be just the ticket to making your quilt eye-catching and memorable.

- Prewash your fabrics. It is much easier to prewash your fabrics than to endure the heartbreak of unexpected and disastrous shrinkages and dye-runs.

Let the theme of this book, houses and feeders "For the Birds," be a major determinant when selecting your fabrics:

Bird prints. Today we are very fortunate to find many of these available, from hummingbirds to cardinals to robins. What is even better is that many are printed with enough surrounding background area between each bird to "fussy-cut" them and use them in corner posts and corner blocks (see "Springtime Delight" on page 93). Or add a bit of whimsy to your house by having a bird peeking out from the entry hole.

Wood and leaf prints. Most birdhouses and bird feeders can be found hanging outside under the branches and leaves of trees, so you'll want to add a good supply of brown woodgrain prints and leaf prints to your stash. You can never have too many leaf prints or too many shades of green.

Background skies. Many of the blocks use blue as the background sky, but don't forget the nighttime sky or the sky of an overcast day. Note the pale yellow sunshine cast of "Springtime Delight" (page 93). In order to bring out the fresh sunlight of spring, a creamy yellow fabric was used rather than the brighter, clearer blue as in the summer sky of "It's a Birds' Picnic in the Park" (page 90).

Structure prints. Look for prints that suggest woodgrain, old peeling paint cracks (worn and natural), wood planks or boards, shingles and roof tiles, woven basketry, and reeds and grasses. Be imaginative and creative in your search. Avoid purchasing large amounts of a few pieces and choose instead to gather small amounts of many prints.

Seeds. Fabrics that depict or convey the look of seeds can be the hardest to find, so when you do locate one, forget my previous advice and get plenty! Of course, don't ask for "seed" fabric, but rather position your fingers and hands into a "viewing square" as shown on page 8. Do not look only at the overall print, but focus on a small area and find a part of the print that could be birdseed.

CONSTRUCTION TERMINOLOGY

It is helpful to have a common understanding of the construction terminology used whenever you embark on a new project. It guarantees that the builder—the sewer—is interpreting the information the same way as the architect—the designer. It is everyone's goal that the birdhouse or feeder that is being built is indeed like the design and model shown.

This section contains brief definitions of the various terms and phrases encountered when using paper foundation piecing to construct the buildings. Several definitions contain specific page references to more complete, detailed explanations.

Accent border. A reference to the use of the ¼"-wide border presented in "Framing Your Projects" (page 15).

Dashed lines. Marks used to separate the pattern parts (page 10). Compare to "Solid Lines."

Fabric key. The table provided with each pattern that lists all fabrics needed. Each fabric is identified by a capital letter, while the sewing-order designations are indicated with a boldface letter.

Foundation pattern. That pattern on which you actually sew. It contains the sewing lines and parts, as well as the fabric symbols. It can be a variety of forms, but the recommended type in this book is commercially available freezer paper.

Hash marks or **reference marks.** Pre-sewing marks that are added to your foundation pattern on every dashed line. The rule is, "dashes need hashes." Later, these reference marks will be used to pinpoint match your parts together exactly (page 14).

Paper foundation piecing. An organized step-by-step process of piecing fabrics together in alphabetic and numeric order directly onto a foundation on which the sewing lines have been drawn. Refer to "Steps to Successful Paper Foundation Piecing" (page 9).

Part. An organized collection of pattern pieces, separated from each other on the pattern by short dashed lines.

Piece. The smallest unit within a pattern. It makes use of only one fabric piece.

Form a square with your hands to focus on just part of a print.

Pin-checking. A quick test to see if enough fabric has been allowed for flipping up later with complete coverage of a particular pattern piece. It involves pinning along the proposed sewing line and then checking by flipping up the new fabric piece to see if the additional fabric will be large enough (page 12).

Pinpoint matching. A technique for ensuring that the pattern parts are correctly aligned. Using the hash marks, poke a sewing pin straight through the top of a hash mark and into the fabric of one part, then into the corresponding hash mark of the part you are attaching. If correctly aligned, they will match (page 14).

Reverse or mirror image. This is the orientation of the foundation pattern. It is the wrong side of the finished project. The design on the foundation appears as a reverse image of the final project.

Sewing order. The step-by-step listing of the order in which you sew or piece the pattern. It is the alphabetic and numeric blueprint to the piecing of each pattern (i.e., Part A: 1–4.)

Solid lines. Used to indicate separate pattern pieces within parts. Solid lines indicate sewing lines. Do not cut along these lines.

Staystitching. Stabilizing the outer edges of your pattern block with a line of stitching ⅛" from the edge. It keeps the bias edges of your block or wall hanging from stretching until you can add borders or binding.

Building Birdhouses and Feeders

Every block presented in this book follows the same paper-piecing construction steps. It's a simple process of following an alphabetic and numeric sewing order. Specific directions for pattern preparation, precision pin-matching, and parts assembly are included in "Steps to Successful Paper Foundation Piecing" below.

Following the directions for paper foundation piecing, you will find directions for creating accurate ¼" borders to effectively "frame up" your houses and feeders, block arrangements for a variety of looks, and surface enhancements for "fine finishes."

As the "general contractor" on these building projects, take a few moments to read over the directions, perhaps even sew one of the smaller 4" companion blocks as a test piece, and make sure you understand each step in the process. We all want our birdhouses and feeders to be "built solidly," as well as to look good for the bird sanctuaries inside our homes.

STEPS TO SUCCESSFUL PAPER FOUNDATION PIECING

Step 1: Make A Swatch Chart

The first step in the paper-foundation-piecing process is an organizational one: Make a fabric swatch chart for easier fabric control and identification. Although you may be tempted to skip this step, don't! It pays for itself later when many different piles of colored fabrics and scraps surround you and you cannot remember which green is the particular one you need. Also, as the patterns become more elaborate and you need more fabrics, it becomes more difficult to keep track of them all. The swatch chart can bring some order to the chaos!

Choose a fabric for each element of your project; then tape, glue, pin, or staple a small swatch of each to a piece of paper. Add identifying labels, including the appropriate pattern-piece letter, beneath each swatch.

The rule to remember is "Check your swatch chart twice, sew only once." This is a good rule to follow with any sewing project.

Step 2: Trace the Pattern onto the Foundation

Trace the desired block pattern onto your paper foundation. You have several choices of material to use for the foundation, including standard typing paper, bleached newsprint, tear-away stabilizer, or freezer paper. I recommend commercially available freezer paper because of its superior adhering qualities. After you iron the fabrics to it, they tend to remain tidily tucked out of the way. (The directions assume you will use a freezer-paper foundation, but they also apply if you use another foundation material.)

This book includes a foundation pattern for each block design. The foundation pattern has all parts labeled with the sewing order and fabric designations. This is the pattern on which you actually sew. Notice that it is the mirror image of the finished block; everything appears in reverse order. This is as it should be, because you sew on the wrong side, or the paper side.

When you turn your work over to the fabric side, you see that everything is correct.

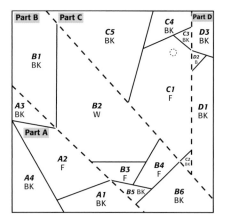

Foundation Pattern

When tracing your foundation pattern, it is helpful to use a light table or tape your pattern to a window. If you have a table with a center leaf, make your own light table by removing the leaf, placing a piece of glass across the opening, and putting a lamp underneath. If you are using freezer paper, remember to trace the pattern on the paper side, not the shiny, plastic-coated side.

After tracing all the lines (both straight and dashed), be sure to re-label and re-number each piece carefully and accurately. Please note that the alphabetic and numeric designations provide you with the sewing order (A1, D5, E4) in boldface letters, while the smaller letters indicate fabric (for example, "BK" means to use the fabric designated for the background).

When you have finished tracing, cut out the entire pattern or block. Trim away any excess foundation paper from the outer edges.

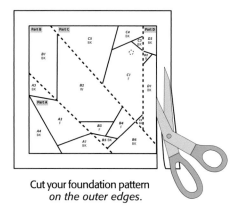

Cut your foundation pattern
on the outer edges.

Some of the quilts in this book use mirror images of the block designs. To make a mirror image of a block, place the pattern right side down on a light table or other light source. Place the freezer paper, shiny side down, directly over the foundation pattern. Trace all the lines, dashes (both long and short), sewing order numbers, and fabric designations exactly as given. Be sure to reverse the numbers so that they are readable.

Step 3: Add Reference Marks to Your Foundation

Adding reference marks, or hash marks, to your foundation is another step that should be preceded by the words "Do it now because it more than pays for itself later!" Trust me on this.

On each pattern solid lines or dashed lines separate individual pieces and parts. Solid lines separate pattern pieces within parts. Do not cut along these lines with the exception of the outer edge of the pattern itself. These are your sewing lines. Short dashed lines separate parts of the pattern within particular blocks. Later you will be cutting the parts apart along the dashed lines. Long dashed lines represent cutting lines between pattern sections.

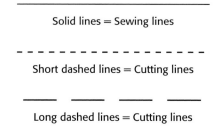

Solid lines = Sewing lines

Short dashed lines = Cutting lines

Long dashed lines = Cutting lines

Every dashed line should have reference marks added across it. These marks will later serve as the precise matching points between parts when joining them together. Remember the rule: Dashes need hashes. If it is a dashed line, it should receive reference marks. Make use of many different types of reference marks—single slash, double slash, triple slash, single X, double X, etc.

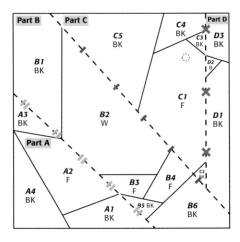

Any marking tool is acceptable, but be sure to use several different colors so matching is easier. Avoid yellow—it's difficult to read. I find that Crayola thin-line washable markers work well.

Step 4: Refer to the Sewing Order

Every pattern comes with a Sewing Order. This is a step-by-step listing of the exact order in which to piece or sew the pattern. It tells you what you should sew first, and what to do with it when it is finished. It tells you when to join various parts together. It is basically a construction plan to the piecing of each pattern, giving you the correct piecing and placement order.

As you follow the Sewing Order, place a check mark before each step as you complete it. This becomes a handy reference for knowing where you were when you stopped last.

✔ Part A: 1–4
✔ Part B: 1–6
   Join A to B (AB)
   Part C: 1–5
   Part D: 1–3
   Join C to D (CD)
   Join AB to CD (ABCD)

Step 5: Cut Out the First Part

After consulting the Sewing Order, locate the first part listed. Remember, in paper foundation piecing you work both alphabetically and numerically. The more complicated the pattern, the more parts there will be. Your Sewing Order will tell you what is first. Whatever it is, find the first part on your foundation and with your scissors, carefully cut it out. Attempt to cut exactly on the line. Remember, cut only on dashed lines, not on straight lines. Set the rest of the foundation sheet aside.

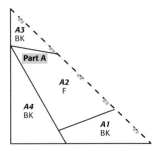

Chickadee block: Part A

Step 6: Iron the First Piece

Locate the first piece, A1, and its corresponding fabric (check your swatch chart). From your fabric, roughly cut out a piece large enough to cover that area completely with at least a $\frac{1}{4}$" seam allowance all around. When in doubt, err on the side of too large. With the wrong side of the fabric to the shiny side of the freezer paper, iron the first piece in place.

NOTE: This is the only piece that is ironed in place before it is sewn.

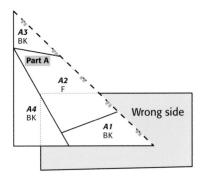

Step 7: Begin Sewing

Look at your foundation to determine which fabric is indicated for the second piece. After consulting your swatch chart, cut a piece of fabric large enough to cover the piece. Do not try to cut fabrics the exact size of the piece. Instead, use large enough pieces to ensure coverage, with extra for seam allowance. You will be trimming away the excess and frequently can use the leftovers in another place.

In this process do not concern yourself with grain line. If such concern is important, indicate the direction on your foundation with an arrow and carefully adjust the fabric placement so the grain line is aligned with that arrow.

Hold the foundation so the paper side is facing you and the attached fabric piece #1 is behind it. Rotate the paper so that A1 is below A2. Locate your sewing line. It is the solid line running between piece #1 and piece #2. Right sides together, place fabric piece #2 over piece #1 with at least ¼" of fabric extending beyond the sewing line. With the foundation paper side facing you, hold the whole unit up to the light to see if you must reposition your fabric. At this point, most of piece #2 will be behind piece #1.

NOTE: The previously sewn work will always be below the line on which you are sewing.

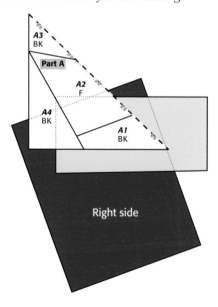

Right side

Again, make sure that the fabric piece you are adding will be large enough to cover the area it is designed to cover, plus extra for seam allowance. Too big is better than too small. It is better to waste a bit of fabric than to have to remove stitches and start

again. If you are unsure whether your new piece is large enough, test it first. Simply pin the new fabric along the proposed sewing line and flip the fabric up. You can now truly see whether it is the correct size. This takes only a few seconds but is well worth the effort. (Pin-checking takes a lot less time than ripping out fifteen to twenty stitches per inch!)

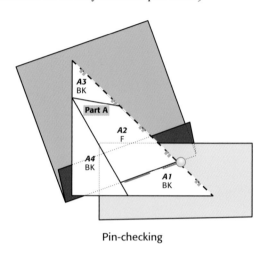

Pin-checking

With the foundation paper side up, sew along the length of the seam over the pattern line, using fifteen to twenty stitches per inch. Backstitch if desired. The purpose of such small stitches is to make the removal of the paper foundation easier.

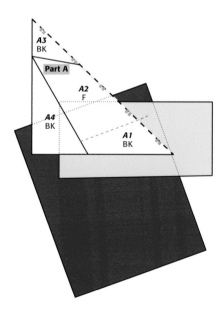

Step 8: Trim the Seam Allowance

Remove the unit from the machine and lay it flat on the table with the foundation side up. With your fingers holding down the previously sewn fabrics that are still right sides together, carefully fold back the foundation at the sewing line. Using your thumbnail, crease the foundation paper along the sewing line. Do not flip up the fabrics yet. Pick up the unit and trim the fabric layers to a scant ¼" seam allowance. Use a small pair of scissors and simply eyeball the ¼" trim, or use a rotary cutter and ruler if desired.

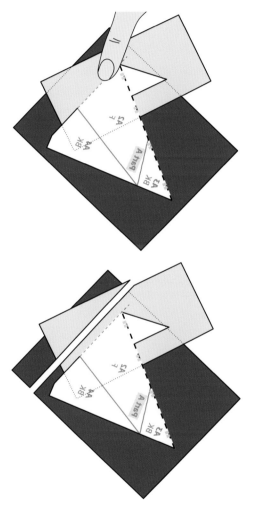

Step 9: Flip and Press

Once you have trimmed the fabric, fold the foundation paper back down. Flip up the newly attached fabric piece and iron it into place, ensuring a sharp, creased fold along the seam line. Press from the paper side first, gently pulling on the new fabric piece as you glide the iron toward your hand and over the paper. Then flip the whole unit over and press from the fabric side. This allows you to check for excess fabric folds or pleats on the seam line.

Check to make sure the entire pattern piece is covered with plenty of extra fabric around the sewing lines. This excess is your seam allowance. If you have lots of excess fabric, carefully trim it away, but make sure you leave plenty around the outer edges of the piece. Keep the trimmed pieces for possible use later for smaller pattern pieces.

This is where the advantage of freezer paper's adhering quality is very apparent. The freezer paper holds the fabrics exactly where you have pressed them and keeps them out of your way.

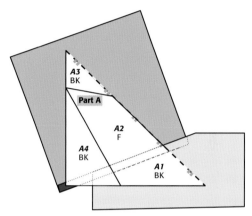

Step 10: Repeat the Process

Continue in this manner until the entire part is completed. With each new fabric piece, refer to step 7. Remember to sew the pieces in numeric order, or they won't fit together correctly. Continue with step 11 once the entire part has been sewn.

Step 11: Trim the Finished Part

Once a part has been finished, trim an exact ¼" seam allowance around all of the sides. As accuracy counts here, use your rotary cutter, mat, and ruler. Do not eyeball this seam allowance.

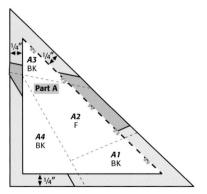

Next, check the Sewing Order. You may be instructed to set this part aside, to go on to the next part, or to join parts together. It all depends on where you are on the pattern.

Step 12: Join the Parts

Once several parts are complete, it is necessary to join them together accurately and precisely. This is where those reference marks from step 3 really pay off.

First, carefully align the appropriate parts with their corresponding reference marks (i.e., single red slashes align to single red slashes; double blues with double blues, etc.). Hold them with the fabric right sides together.

Next, pinpoint match the reference mark. Insert a pin through the hash mark on one part, then through the fabrics and into the paper of the other part. Ideally, the pin will line up exactly and pierce the corresponding mark on the other piece. If it does not, simply reposition the pin until it does. Remember, these are bias edges, so they will ease right in. Add as many pins along an edge as needed for exact placement.

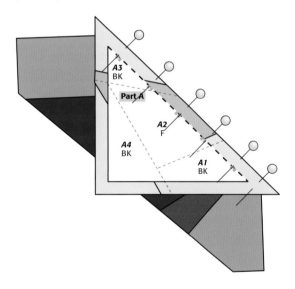

Sew along the pinned edge. The needle should just barely brush the paper's edge. Sew carefully,

slowly, and accurately. Do not remove the pins until the last moment, or you will lose your perfect match as the pieces shift or slide away from each other.

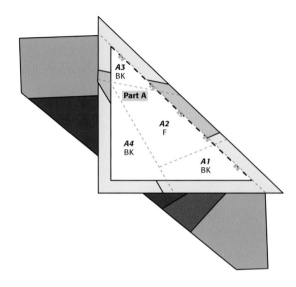

Remove the unit from the sewing machine and check to make sure the points match precisely.

Step 13: Press the Seam Allowances

Once the parts are sewn together, press the seam allowances. The general rule is to let them go where they want to go. Press toward the direction of least resistance. If needed, press the seam allowances open to spread out the bulk of several parts coming together at the same point. Continue in this manner until all parts are completely joined together, checking the Sewing Order for guidance.

Step 14: Remove the Paper

Do not remove the foundation paper from the outside edges of a part until it has been joined to other parts or until the outer edges have been joined to sashing or borders. Remember, these fabrics have been cut and placed with no real concern for grain line, so the edges are primarily bias edges and can easily stretch or become distorted. To control this, staystitch $\frac{1}{8}$" from the finished block or pattern edges.

Once the part is stabilized by other parts or outer borders, gently remove the foundation paper. Usually the smaller stitch length allows for easy removal, but with tightly adhered pieces, use a stiletto. Gently insert the stiletto point between the paper and fabric and carefully ease it between them, going back and forth to loosen the paper. It may also help to gently bend or roll the paper and fabric unit, loosening the bond between them. Avoid tugging or tearing too hard on the seam lines and stitches.

Be sure to remove all pieces of the foundation, using tweezers to remove paper from tiny corners or crevices.

Step 15: Add Sashing and Borders

The first border or sashing is the most important one because it stabilizes your paper-foundation-pieced project and corrals all those tiny bits and pieces.

The beauty of paper foundation piecing should be readily apparent in this step because your blocks and designs are truly accurate. If sewn correctly, your points will be almost perfect, and there will be $\frac{1}{4}$" seam allowances all around. The side measurements should all match, so adding sashing and simple borders becomes a breeze!

For more information on adding borders, refer to "Framing Your Projects" at right.

FRAMING YOUR PROJECTS

Once your structure is sewn, it becomes important to consider the best way to set it off with sashing and borders. Just as a builder becomes concerned with the curb appeal created by the landscaping, walkways, and fencing, you need to provide the best "look" for the areas surrounding your blocks.

One suggestion is to frame the block or a group of blocks with one or more narrow borders that effectively surround your work and set it apart, very much like fencing or landscape shrubbery. Each of the blocks for the individual structures are shown with the $\frac{1}{4}$" framing border, as well as several of the larger projects (refer to "All Around the Neighborhood" on page 74 and "Home for the Holidays" on page 87).

The following steps allow you to easily create very accurate $\frac{1}{4}$"-wide framing borders for your blocks. Pay particular attention to step 4, which shows how to establish your sewing line from an inside seam rather than from the outside fabric edges.

Step 1: Square-Up

The process begins by first squaring up your project, whether it is a pieced block, a fussy-cut picture from a pre-printed fabric, or even a small wall hanging ready to have borders added.

Using your rotary cutter and a ruler with right angles (a $12\frac{1}{2}$" x $12\frac{1}{2}$" ruler works well), square-up the work, making sure you have straight sides and accurate 90° angles in each corner.

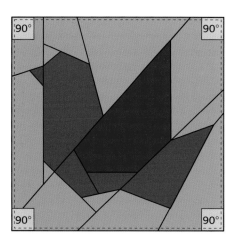

Step 2: Cut the "Framing" Border Strips

Next, cut ¾"-wide strips from the fabric to be used as your framing border.

Step 3: Cut Other Border Strips

Cut the border that follows the framing border the width desired plus ½". For instance, if you wish the next border to finish to 2", cut your strips 2½" wide. Set these aside.

Step 4: Create the Framing Border

Framing borders are created using the straight-set technique, so first you must decide the order you are going to use when attaching the border strips (i.e., side-side-top-bottom, or top-bottom-side-side). Neither is better nor more correct than the other, but once you choose an order, remain consistent for all the remaining borders you add. For our purposes here, we are showing a single block with the framing strips added to the top and bottom first, then the sides.

1. Using a ¼" seam allowance, stitch a ¾" wide framing strip to the top and bottom of the pieced project.

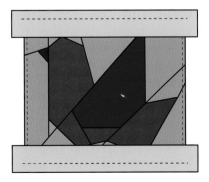

2. Press the stitches flat to set them, and then press the seam allowances toward the center of the project.

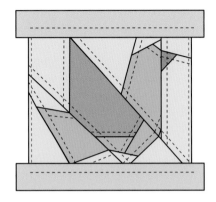

— TIP —

Pressing toward the center will tend to bury the ¼" border. If you press the seam allowances away from the project, the framing border will stand up over the project, much like actual framing mats do in a picture. The choice is yours.

3. Trim the strip ends even with the project sides to square up the project again.

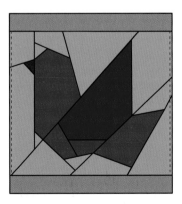

4. Add the remaining two framing strips to the project sides. Press and trim in the same manner as the top and bottom borders.

5. Working on the wrong side of the project, draw lines to extend the top and bottom strip seam lines to the strip edges. These lines will become the sewing guidelines rather than the outer edges.

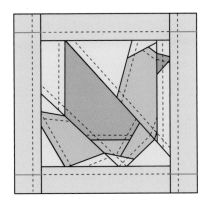

6. Locate the $\frac{1}{4}$" guide on your presser foot as shown. You may also use an actual $\frac{1}{4}$" presser foot or simply measure and mark the width on your presser foot. Some machines also allow you to move your needle position.

$\frac{1}{4}$" guide

7. Pick up a strip of your next border. Remember, you are adding the borders top-bottom-side-side, so your first addition will be the top strip. With right sides together and edges aligned, place the new border strip under the center unit so you can see the marked guidelines you have drawn. Stitch the top border strip to the framing border, stitching $\frac{1}{4}$" from the *previous seam line and extension line*, not the outside edges you normally follow.

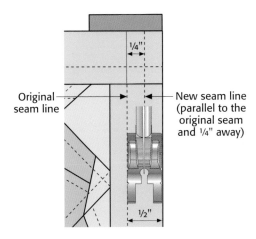

Original seam line

New seam line (parallel to the original seam and $\frac{1}{4}$" away)

$\frac{1}{4}$"

$\frac{1}{2}$"

Press the seam flat, then away from the center of the project. Add the bottom strip and trim the ends even with the sides. When finished, look at your work. Now you can see where the sewing lines run parallel only $\frac{1}{4}$" apart.

8. After the top and bottom framing borders have been added, turn the block to the wrong side and draw in the new extension lines for the side strips.

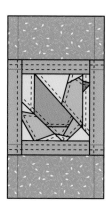

9. Add the side strips; trim the ends even with the top and bottom. Turn your work over and look at the right side. Look at that accurate, wonderful, ¼" border!

— TIP —

Don't be concerned with how accurate or even the seam allowances are on the back. Concentrate on how even the border appears on the front of the quilt top and how dramatic it looks.

Step 5: Add Remaining Borders

Continue in this manner with any remaining borders. To finish your project with a mitered outer border, refer to the following instructions.

Making Borders with Mitered Corners

1. Cut the border strips as indicated in the cutting directions for each quilt.

2. On the quilt, mark the center of each side of the quilt top. Mark the ¼" seam intersections on the 4 quilt corners.

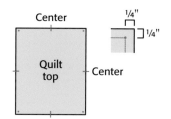

3. Mark the center of each border strip and ¼" in from where the corners of the quilt will be.

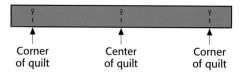

4. With right sides together, pin the side border strips to the quilt sides, matching center and corner marks. Stitch from corner mark to corner mark. Press the seam allowances toward the border. Repeat for the top and bottom borders, making sure the stitching lines meet exactly at the corners.

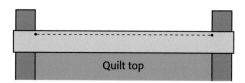

5. With right sides together, fold the quilt diagonally so that the border strips are aligned. Using a ruler with a 45° angle, draw a line on the wrong side of the border strip from the corner mark to the outside edge as shown.

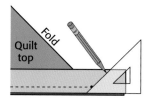

6. Pin the borders together and stitch on the drawn line. Open out the top and make sure the seam is flat and accurate before trimming the seam allowances. Press the seam open. Repeat for the remaining corners.

FINE FINISHES

When constructing any building project, it is important to remember the finishing details. It is these touches that often separate fine craftsmanship from the average workmanship of others. Just as the traditional builder must be concerned with sanding, polishing, painting, and landscaping, we, as builders with thread and fabric, must be concerned with our fine finishes as well. It is the quality workmanship and the loving care of the final details that will make our quilts special. In the case of these birdhouses and feeders, fine finishes include the basting and the quilting, the embellishments (buttons, beads, embroidery, appliqué), the binding and rod pocket, and the label. We, too, want to create "positive curb appeal" for our houses and feeders.

Embellishing

Embellishment details add whimsy and fun to the basic blocks. They are what beckon the viewer to come closer for a more careful study and examination and perhaps even a touch. Add embroidery and appliqué details after assembling the quilt top; add buttons and beads after quilting.

Buttons

Calling all you button lovers! These birdhouse blocks and quilts are made for you. Run to your collection of buttons and dig your fingers in, searching for that perfect button. The large round or oval buttons can easily become entry holes, and the tiny little ones can serve as perches, while those funny rectangular buttons could be perfect landing ledges.

Wherever you find them, whatever their color or shape, consider each button carefully and choose them specifically to enhance your blocks and quilts. They truly can provide that "special added value!"

Seed Beads

There are also instances where the addition of small seed beads adds to the realism of the block. The bird blocks require eyes, and black seed beads are suggested to serve the purpose. In addition to eyes, the seed beads can also be used to simulate nail heads. Look closely at the tall "Pole Birdhouse" (page 57) or "Rustic Cabin Birdhouse" (page 29). Each can be enhanced by the use of small seed beads to represent nail heads.

Normally you want your seed beads to stand up on their sides, but for the quilts in this book, the beads will look more like an actual eye or nail head if they lie flat so you can see the center opening of the bead. Follow the illustration below to stitch the beads so they lie flat.

Embroidery

Adding some simple hand embroidery stitches such as the basic stem stitch or the buttonhole stitch can further enhance several of the designs. This can be especially useful if a bit more contrast is needed between your fabrics. A simple outline of an edge or part can effectively separate the shapes. Refer to "Stem Stitch and Blanket Stitch" on page 20 to make these stitches.

Remember, these fabric pieces and blocks are delicate. Try not to stretch your blocks or pull the embroidery thread too tight as you stitch.

For those of you fortunate to have the use of a home embroidery machine, these blocks and quilts can be an excellent place to display your work, either within the blocks themselves, or on additional/alternate blocks. Look closely at "At Home in the Rose Garden" (page 78) where many types of machine-embroidered leaves were sewn into each background triangle of the alternate Hourglass blocks. The thread colors chosen came from the color palette within the white rose border print. Many different leaf designs were stitched and then incorporated throughout the quilt. Further, notice the small wrens that appear in the corners of this quilt. What an abundant choice of home, shelter, and food these four small birds enjoy! Wouldn't you feel at home in this rose garden?

To make a stem stitch

1. On your pieced block, lightly draw the desired design lines with a water-soluble marker or a pencil.
2. Cut off an 18" length of embroidery thread or floss in the desired color. Separate the 6 strands into 2-strand lengths.
3. Thread the needle with a 2-strand length and knot the end.
4. Insert the needle into the fabric from the back to the front at point A. As you begin, bury the knot, if possible, behind some darker fabric or else gently weave the end into the stitches as you work.
5. Insert the needle at point B and then come out at point C. Repeat to the end of the drawn line, spacing the stitches evenly. Always keep the thread below or to the right of the needle.

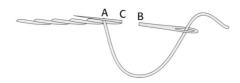

6. Bury the thread end by reweaving it into the stitching on the fabric wrong side.

To make a blanket stitch

1. Cut off an 18" length of embroidery thread or floss in the desired color. Separate the 6 strands into 2-strand lengths.
2. Thread the needle with a 2-strand length and knot the end.
3. Bring the needle to the right side of the fabric at along the edge to be finished. Working from left to right, hold the thread down and insert the needle into the fabric at B and out below the edge at C. Draw the thread through the loop that has been

formed. Continue making stitches along the edge, keeping the space between the stitches even.

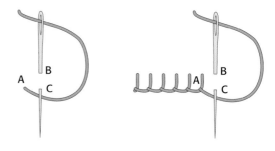

4. When the last stitch has been formed, take several small stitches on the back of the project to secure the stitching.

Appliqué

Consider using some appliqué to add detail to your structures. For instance, the butterfly house needs some butterflies fluttering about. Butterfly buttons can do this quite effectively, but another alternative is to use a beautifully colored butterfly fabric. Fussy-cut a few of the butterflies, and then appliqué them to your blocks using your favorite hand or machine appliqué method. This technique also applies to bird print fabrics. Wouldn't a tiny bird look cute peeking out from one of the houses? Or a pair of birds feeding at one of the feeders? Or perhaps several flying around the structures?

If you choose not to use buttons for the birdhouse openings, feel free to use a fabric appliqué instead. Simply use the dotted line markings on the foundation pattern as a guide for making the appliqué template (be sure to add seam allowance if hand appliquéing) and stitch the motif in place using your favorite hand or machine appliqué method.

Basting

Before you begin quilting, the three layers of your quilt (the pieced top, the batting, and the backing) must be anchored together. The careful basting you do now leads to easier quilting later.

1. Prewash the backing fabric and batting if needed or desired. Check the batting manufacturer's instructions, as well.

2. Cut the backing fabric and batting 4" to 6" larger than the pieced top. This allows for some drawing up of the top as you quilt or for some shifting and movement of the top.

3. Build the layers from the bottom up. First, place the backing fabric right side down on the table or other flat work surface. Secure it with masking tape in several places along the edges. Second, place the batting on top of the secured backing. It, too, can be secured with masking tape if needed. Third, center the pieced top, right side up, onto the batting and backing. Carefully smooth it out from the center.

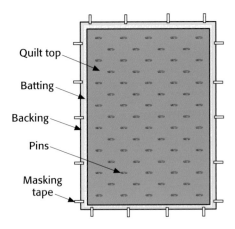

Quilt top

Batting

Backing

Pins

Masking tape

4. Baste the layers together, using thread for hand quilting or size 0 or 1 rustproof safety pins for machine quilting (recommended). Space pins about 3" to 4" apart and $1/4$" away from the area you intend to quilt.

Quilting

Paper foundation piecing is a great technique for producing detailed blocks, but while the end result is accuracy, there are often a number of seam allowances that are close together. For this reason, I recommend machine quilting these blocks. Hand quilting would be very time consuming as well as hard on the fingers. Following are some suggestions for machine quilting specific areas and parts.

- *The structures.* Quilt "in the ditch" around the outline of each feeder or house, around each

component of a structure (i.e., the perches, roof levels, etc.), and around each leaf and branch. This causes the angles and edges of each piece to stand out more clearly and precisely. Within each block, quilt each component as if it were only one piece of the same fabric. For example, the siding of a house may be composed of three small pieces but it should be quilted as one larger piece. However, if a component is composed of several different fabrics (i.e., the different colored planks of the "Rustic Cabin Birdhouse" on page 29), separate, and thus emphasize, each fabric piece (i.e., each plank) by quilting in the ditch around each one.

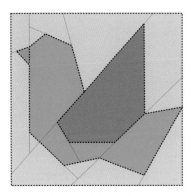

In-the-ditch quilting

- *The background sky.* In the background of each block, the question becomes "to quilt or not to quilt?" Both choices are appropriate. The backgrounds in the blocks of "All Around the Neighborhood" (page 74) were left unquilted and they look fine. However, in many of the individual wall hangings, the backgrounds were stipple quilted to provide more texture and dimension. Such quilting causes a "bubbly" texture which looks good to the eye, feels good to the touch, and causes the structures themselves to stand out more clearly.

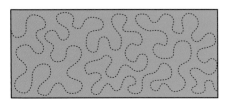

Meandering or stipple quilting

- *Alternate blocks*. Much of the focus of the quilt "At Home in the Rose Garden" (page 78) is on the machine-embroidered leaves of the alternate Hourglass blocks.

The quilting used within each block is a combination of the two previously mentioned quilting methods. Simple in-the-ditch quilting was used around each leaf design, and closely spaced stipple quilting was used in the background. The effect is subtle and does not detract from either the embroidered leaves or the structures. In fact, the quilting adds visible texture to the quilt, even from a distance. As you advance toward the quilt, small details become more apparent and demand attention. And when actually touched, the satiny finish and dimensionality of the leaves are very appealing.

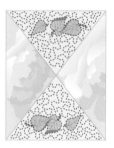

- *Borders*. When quilting the borders, simple parallel lines of quilting are one option. Frequently the width of the walking foot/even-feed foot is used as a guide to evenly space the rows. This type of quilting is used on each of the individual wall quilts to emphasize the border as a "frame" for each structure.

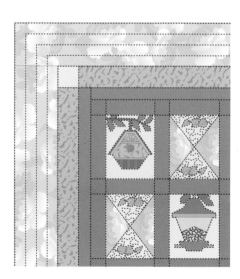

When the outer borders are wider, however, more quilting is recommended. The outer border fabric used in "All around the Neighborhood" (page 74) was so wonderful that it actually determined the quilting. By simply following the lines of the curves and figures within the print, a bit of relief was brought to all the straight-edge piecing within each block and around all the framing borders. To bring even more motion to the quilt and to emphasize the location of these structures as hanging from the trees, the sashing pieces were also quilted using a simple, continuous-line leaf design.

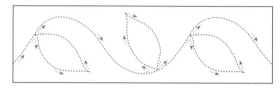

Continue as long as sashing unit length.

Attaching a Rod Pocket

Your quilts will often be displayed hanging on a wall. Follow these steps to make a rod pocket:

1. Measure the width of your quilt at the top and subtract 2". Cut a fabric strip to that length and 5" to 9" wide, depending upon the rod you plan to use for hanging. If needed, cut more than 1 strip and sew the ends together to create the desired length.
2. Press under each end 1/4". Press under again and stitch 1/8" from the first folded edge.

3. Fold the strip in half lengthwise, wrong sides together. Pin it together at the ends and at several points in between. Press.

4. Center the rod pocket on the back of the quilt at the upper edge, aligning raw edges; pin in place. As you add the binding to the upper edge of the quilt, you will automatically attach the rod pocket.

5. After you apply the binding, hand hemstitch the bottom edge of the rod pocket to the quilt back. Be sure to catch only the backing and batting and leave the ends of the sleeve open, sewing only the bottom layer of the rod pocket to the quilt.

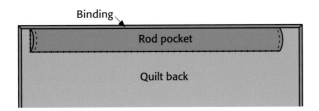

Binding

Binding is a finishing touch that can effectively add to the "curb appeal" of your quilt if done carefully and correctly—but can be disastrous if not. Take the time to give it the attention it deserves. By following the steps given, your binding will be very neat, full of batting, and with "hidden" binding ends.

1. Square up the quilt layers by trimming the excess batting and backing even with the top.

2. Using your rotary-cutting equipment, cut enough 2"-wide strips to go around the quilt, with enough extra for turning corners and joining the ends. Join the strips into one long continuous binding strip using diagonal seams.

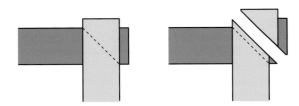

3. Press the binding in half lengthwise, wrong sides and raw edges together.

4. Beginning on one side and leaving an 8" tail at the beginning, place the binding on the quilt top, aligning the binding raw edges with the quilt raw edge. Using a $\frac{1}{4}$" seam allowance, stitch the binding to the quilt top, stopping $\frac{1}{4}$" from the corner. Backstitch and remove the quilt from the machine.

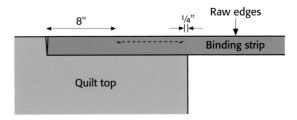

5. With the corner directly in front of you, fold the binding straight up, creating a 45° angle. Then fold the binding straight down, with the fold even with the edges of the quilt. The raw edges of the binding are now even with the next side.

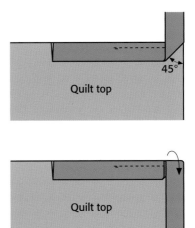

6. Begin stitching just off the fabric at the corner. The new seam is now perpendicular to the previous stitched line. Continue until you are $\frac{1}{4}$" from the next corner and repeat step 5. Repeat for all 4 corners of the quilt, stopping 5" to 10" from where you originally began stitching. Backstitch.

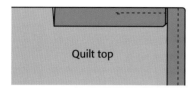

Quilt top

7. Remove the quilt from the machine and leave an 8"-long tail of binding. Lay the quilt flat on the ironing board and carefully fold the 2 tails together at the center. Press, creating easily seen creases.

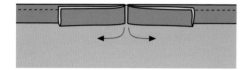

8. Unfold the strip ends. Lay 1 flat, with the right side up. Lay the other, right side down, over it, matching the crease points on the edges. Carefully draw a diagonal line through the point where the fold lines meet. Stitch through the marked line.

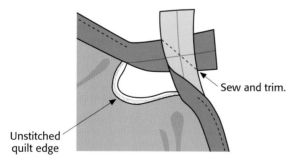

Sew and trim.

Unstitched quilt edge

9. Check to make sure the newly attached binding is the correct length and closes the gap. If so, trim the tails off $\frac{1}{4}$" from the seam. Finger-press the seam allowance open. Refold the binding and finish sewing the binding between the beginning and ending points.

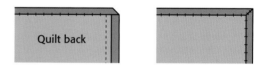

10. Gently bring the binding from the front of the quilt to the back and pin it in place. The binding should easily fold over the seam allowance and just cover the stitching line. Using a thread color that matches the binding, whipstitch the folded edge of the binding to the back of the quilt, being careful that your stitches do not go through to the front of the quilt. As you reach the corners, gently pull the binding straight out. With your thumbnail in the corner, fold over the unstitched binding edge, creating a mitered corner. Secure it with stitching. Do this for all the corners of the quilt.

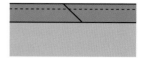

Quilt back

Labeling

One of the fine finishes frequently forgotten is the written description of each quilt, the label. Be sure to include such information as the title of the quilt, the date completed, and your name. But also consider including any important information that provides a more complete story of your quilt. This might include your address and telephone number, the quilt dimensions (width and length), special techniques used (i.e., paper foundation piecing, machine quilting, machine appliqué, etc.), special fabric and/or embellishments used (i.e., batting, fabrics, buttons, etc.), and any special remarks (i.e., for whom the quilt was made, for what special occasion, etc.).

The main point is to document your work for later reference, to give credit where credit is due, to provide a historical document, and thus, to allow future owners to share your quilt's story.

Basic Hanging Birdhouse

This is a birdhouse shape you see quite often. It is not hard to construct and attracts lots of feathered occupants. The style also encourages great use of color to splash across your quilt. "Welcome" could easily be embroidered arching over the entry!

Fabric Key

BK—Background Sky
L1—Leaf 1
L2—Leaf 2
S—Siding
W—Wood Trim

Sewing Order

Part A: 1–9
Part B: 1–16
Part C: 1–4
Part D: 1–3
Join C to D (CD)
Join B to CD (BCD)
Join A to BCD (ABCD)
Part E: 1–6
Join ABCD to E (ABCDE)

Block Embellishment

Sew 1"-diameter button where indicated for bird entry hole.

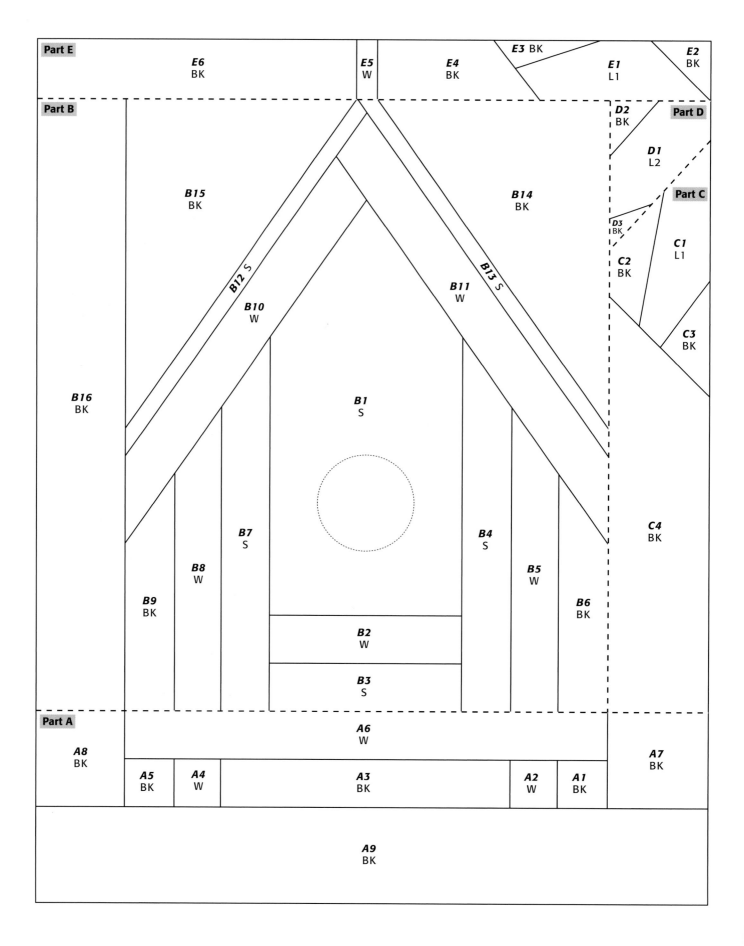

Bungalow Birdhouse

This is probably my favorite bird-house shape—a skewed hexagon. The piecing allows for the use of multiple shades of a color while the graceful shape adds charm to your birdhouse collection. If I were a bird in search of a home, this would be my first choice!

Fabric Key

A—Accent
B—Branch
BK—Background Sky
L1—Leaf 1
L2—Leaf 2
R—Roof
RT—Roof Trim
S1—Siding 1
S2—Siding 2
S3—Siding 3

Sewing Order

Part A: 1–13
Part B: 1–17
Join A to B (AB)
Part C: 1–9
Part D: 1–10
Join C to D (CD)
Part E: 1–4
Part F: 1–5
Part G: 1–4
Join F to G (FG)
Join E to FG (EFG)
Join CD to EFG (CDEFG)
Join AB to CDEFG (ABCDEFG)

Block Embellishments

- Sew 1"-diameter button where indicated for bird entry hole.
- Sew 1/4"-diameter button where indicated for perch.

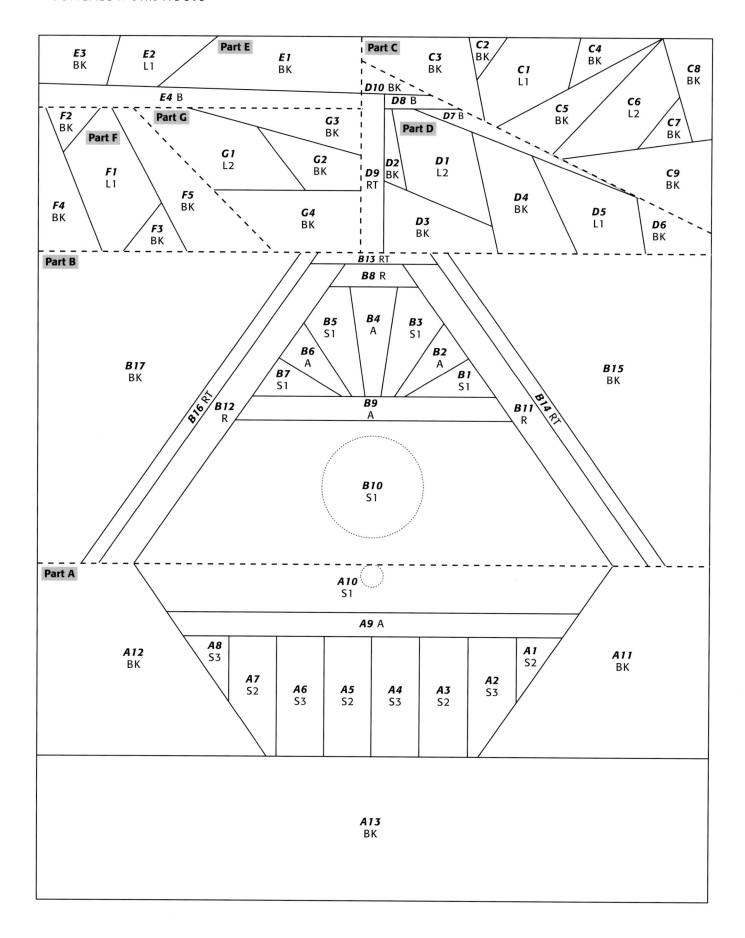

Rustic Cabin Birdhouse

Can't you just picture this house made from old scraps of lumber and leftover boards from past building projects? Turn to your fabric stash of brown, rust, and tan scraps, and "use 'em up" as you build this rustic A-frame cabin for your feathered friends.

Fabric Key	**Sewing Order**	**Block Embellishments**
BK—Background Sky	Part A: 1–15	• Sew 1"-diameter button where indicated for bird entry hole.
DW—Dark Wood	Part B: 1–20	
L1—Leaf 1	Join A to B (AB)	• Sew ¼"-diameter button where indicated for perch.
L2—Leaf 2	Part C: 1–4	
MW—Medium Wood	Part D: 1–5	• Sew seed beads to siding for nail heads.
R—Roof	Join C to D (CD)	
S1—Board 1	Part E: 1–4	
S2—Board 2	Part F: 1–3	
S3—Board 3	Join E to F (EF)	
	Join CD to EF (CDEF)	
	Join AB to CDEF (ABCDEF)	

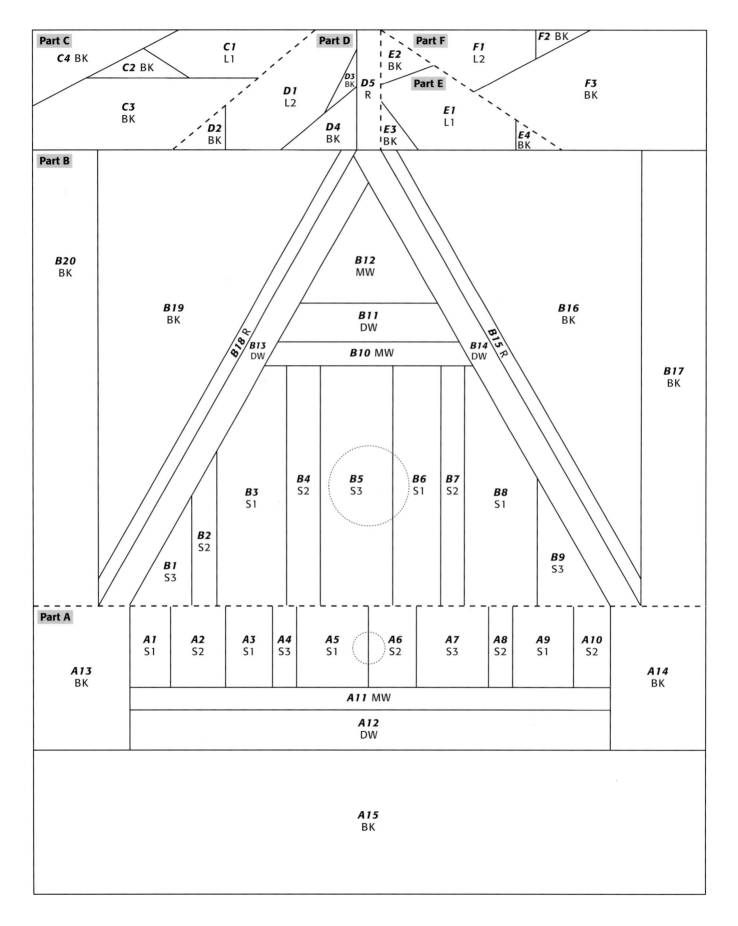

Schoolhouse Birdhouse

Paint this birdhouse a bright school bus yellow and watch the birds flock to it. Let it add a touch of whimsy and character to your collection.

Fabric Key

A—Accent
BK—Background Sky
L1—Leaf 1
L2—Leaf 2
P—Perch
R—Roof
S—Siding
T—Trim

Sewing Order

Part A: 1–7
Part B: 1–10
Part C: 1–7
Join B to C (BC)
Part D: 1–7
Join BC to D (BCD)
Join A to BCD (ABCD)
Part E: 1–7
Part F: 1–3
Join E to F (EF)

Join ABCD to EF (ABCDEF)
Part G: 1–10
Part H: 1–3
Join G to H (GH)
Join ABCDEF to GH (ABCDEFGH)

Block Embellishments

Sew 7/8"-diameter buttons where indicated for bird entry holes.

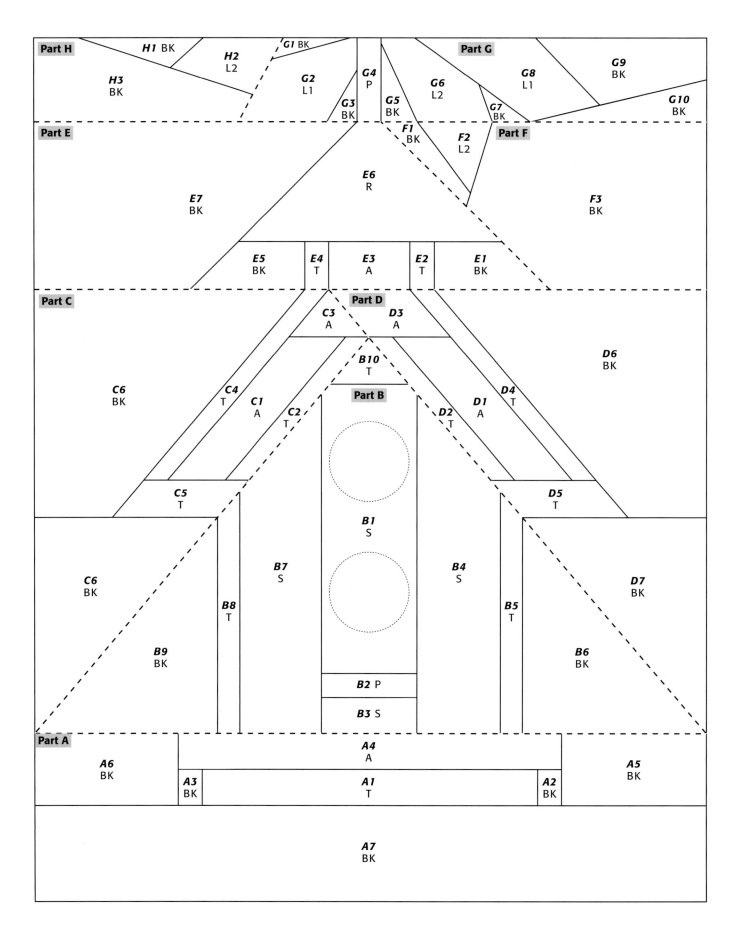

Second Empire-Style Birdhouse

The mansard roof of this birdhouse is what gives this house its style, while the heart-shaped opening adds charm. If "home is where the heart is," then this house is just waiting for a pair of lovebirds to take occupancy. Truly a good place to start a family, wouldn't you say?

Fabric Key

BK—Background Sky
L—Leaf
R—Roof
S—Siding
T—Trim
W—Wire

Sewing Order

Part A: 1–7
Part B: 1–8
Join A to B (AB)
Part C: 1–5
Join AB to C (ABC)
Part D: 1–9
Join ABC to D (ABCD)
Part E: 1–5
Part F: 1–4
Join E to F (EF)
Part G: 1–3
Join EF to G (EFG)
Join ABCD to EFG (ABCDEFG)
Part H: 1–6
Join ABCDEFG to H (ABCDEFGH)

Block Embellishments

- Appliqué hearts (smaller one layered on top of the larger one) where indicated for entry hole (refer to "Appliqué" on page 20).
- Sew ¾"-diameter button where indicated for perch.

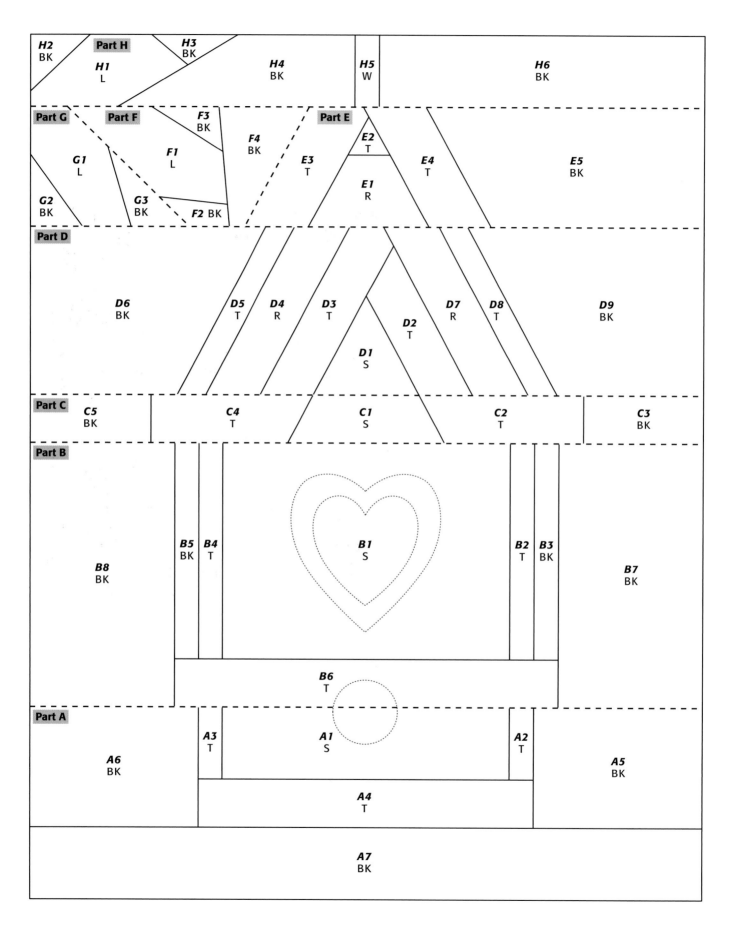

Turret Birdhouse

This birdhouse design was actually inspired by a postage stamp! Don't you just love its gracefully curved roof and rounded shape? Let this house add a unique "touch of class" to the trees and branches of your quilt.

Fabric Key

A1—Accent 1

A2—Accent 2

BK—Background Sky

L1—Leaf 1

L2—Leaf 2

R—Roof

S1—Siding 1

S2—Siding 2

S3—Siding 3

Sewing Order

Part A: 1–6

Part B: 1–3

Join A to B (AB)

Part C: 1–10

Join AB to C (ABC)

Part D: 1–3

Join ABC to D (ABCD)

Part E: 1–5

Join ABCD to E (ABCDE)

Part F: 1–5

Join ABCDE to F (ABCDEF)

Part G: 1–7

Join ABCDEF to G (ABCDEFG)

Part H: 1–7

Join ABCDEFG to H (ABCDEFGH)

Part I: 1–3

Part J: 1–4

Join I to J (IJ)

Join ABCDEFGH to IJ
    (ABCDEFGHIJ)

Block Embellishments

- Sew 7/8"-diameter button where indicated for bird entry hole.
- Sew 3/8"-diameter button where indicated for perch.

- **I3** BK
- ▲ **G2** BK
- ★ **G4** BK

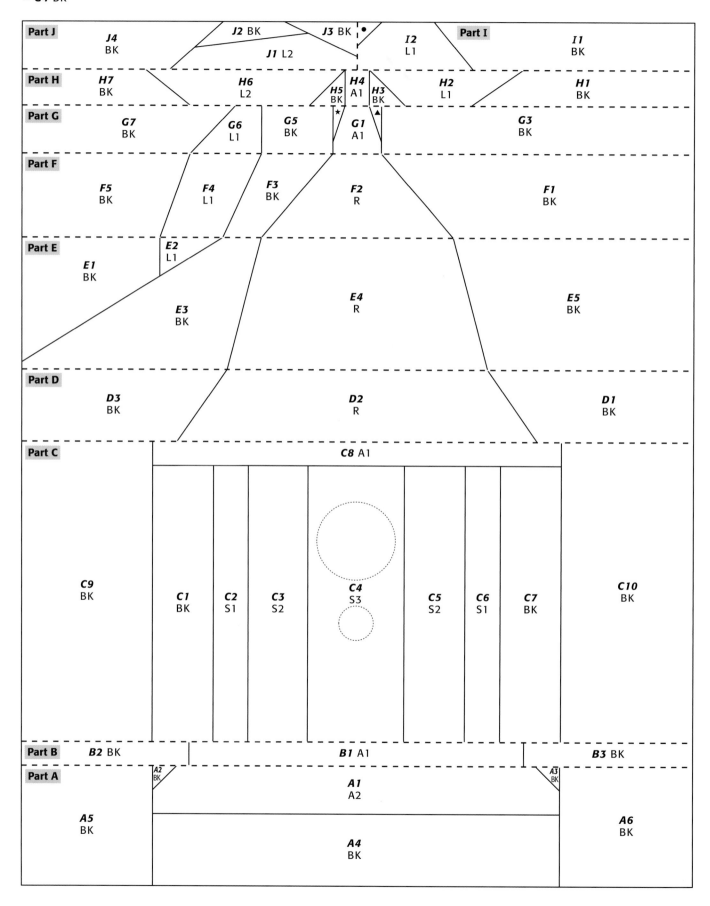

Woven Basket Birdhouse

Look to your fabric stash for those basket weave prints and designs, and use them here. Choose a wonderful accent color in two different shades for a great slanting roof, and suddenly you have an interesting house for your collection.

Fabric Key

B—Branch
BK—Background Sky
L—Leaf
R1—Roof 1
R2—Roof 2
S—Siding
T—Trim

Sewing Order

Part A: 1–6
Part B: 1–5
Join A to B (AB)
Part C: 1–6
Part D: 1–2
Part E: 1–3
Part F: 1–5
Join E to F (EF)
Join D to EF (DEF)
Join C to DEF (CDEF)
Part G: 1–6
Part H: 1–5
Join G to H (GH)
Join CDEF to GH (CDEFGH)
Join AB to CDEFGH (ABCDEFGH)
Part I: 1–5
Part J: 1–4
Join I to J (IJ)
Part K: 1–5
Join IJ to K (IJK)
Join ABCDEFGH to IJK
    (ABCDEFGHIJK)

Block Embellishments

- Appliqué oval where indicated for bird entry hole (refer to "Appliqué" on page 20).
- Sew 3/8"-diameter button where indicated for perch.

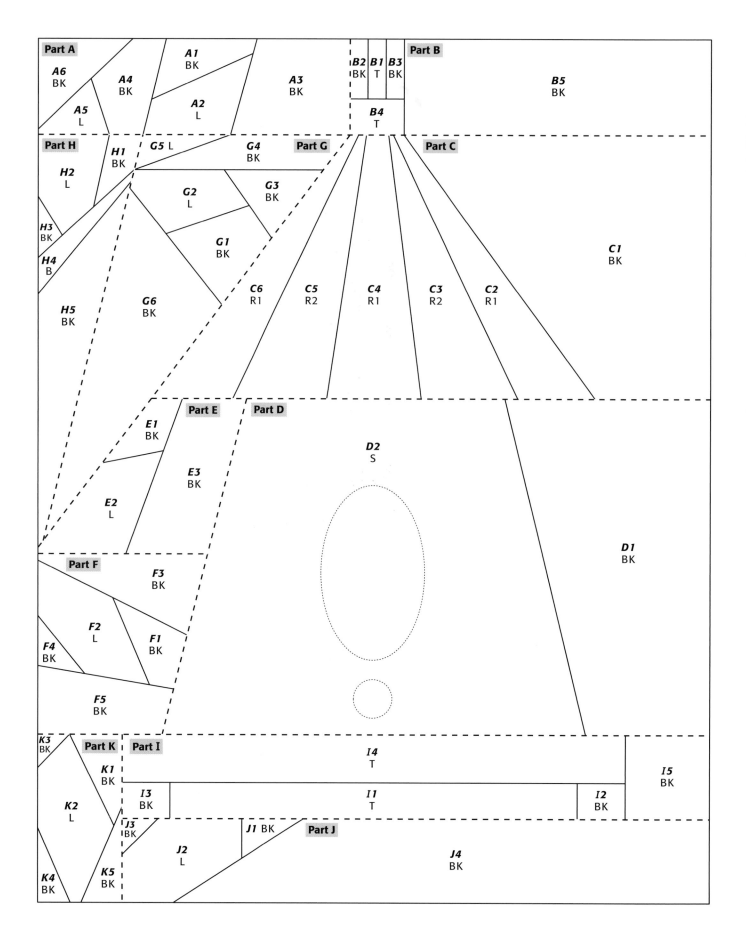

Bottle Bird Feeder

Whether it's an old plastic soda bottle or a fine glass jar, this style of feeder suits many a bird just fine. Bring a spark of interest to your quilt by filling this feeder with "fabric seeds" of wonderful texture and dynamic color, or search for that fabric print that looks "just like the real thing." Whatever you choose, this feeder will be a hit!

Fabric Key

BK—Background Sky
G—Glass
M—Metal Spigot
P—Perch
S—Seeds
T—Trim

Sewing Order

Part A: 1–6
Part B: 1–9
Join A to B (AB)
Part C: 1–6
Join AB to C (ABC)
Part D: 1–4
Part E: 1–6
Join D to E (DE)
Join ABC to DE (ABCDE)

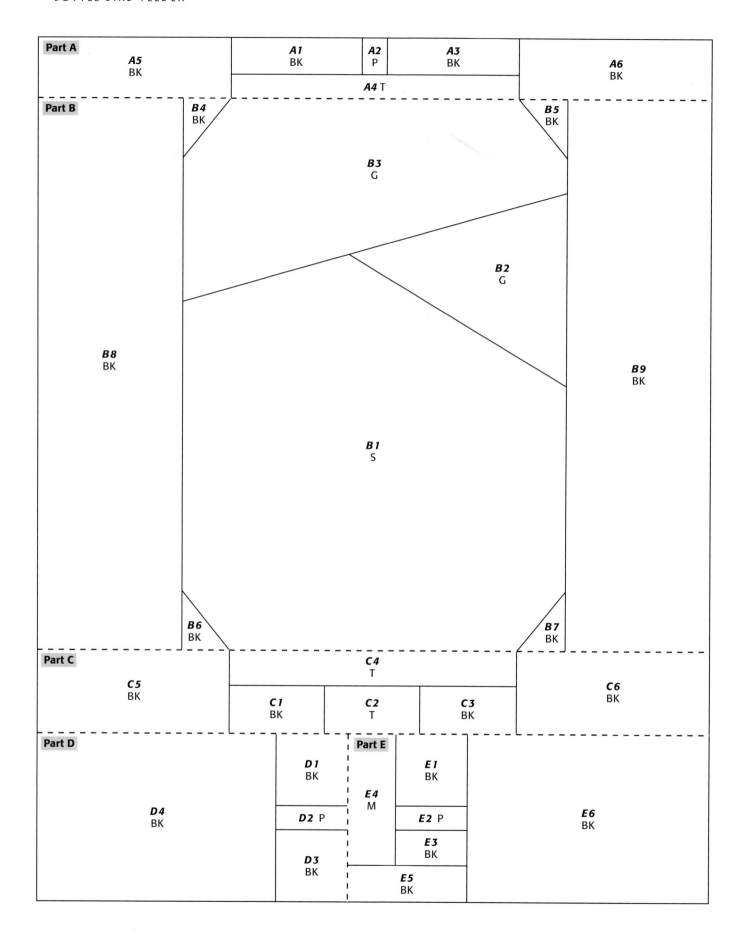

Coach Lantern Bird Feeder

This feeder is very much like the one hanging outside my 99-year-old grandmother's bedroom window. From early morning until late in the day, she enjoys watching the show of activity and color provided by the feathered visitors who stop by. For her, the feeder provides an ever-changing parade of antics and stories to share with others. It doesn't matter whether they are brilliant red cardinals, small brown sparrows, cooing doves, or just plain old grackles—they are all welcome at this feeder.

Fabric Key

B—Base
BK—Background Sky
G—Glass
L1—Leaf 1
L2—Leaf 2
P—Perch
R—Roof
S—Seeds

Sewing Order

Part A: 1–4
Part B: 1–4
Part C: 1–3
Join B to C (BC)
Join A to BC (ABC)
Part D: 1–5
Join ABC to D (ABCD)
Part E: 1–6
Join ABCD to E (ABCDE)
Part F: 1–5
Part G: 1–5
Join F to G (FG)
Join ABCDE to FG (ABCDEFG)
Part H: 1–8
Join ABCDEFG to H (ABCDEFGH)

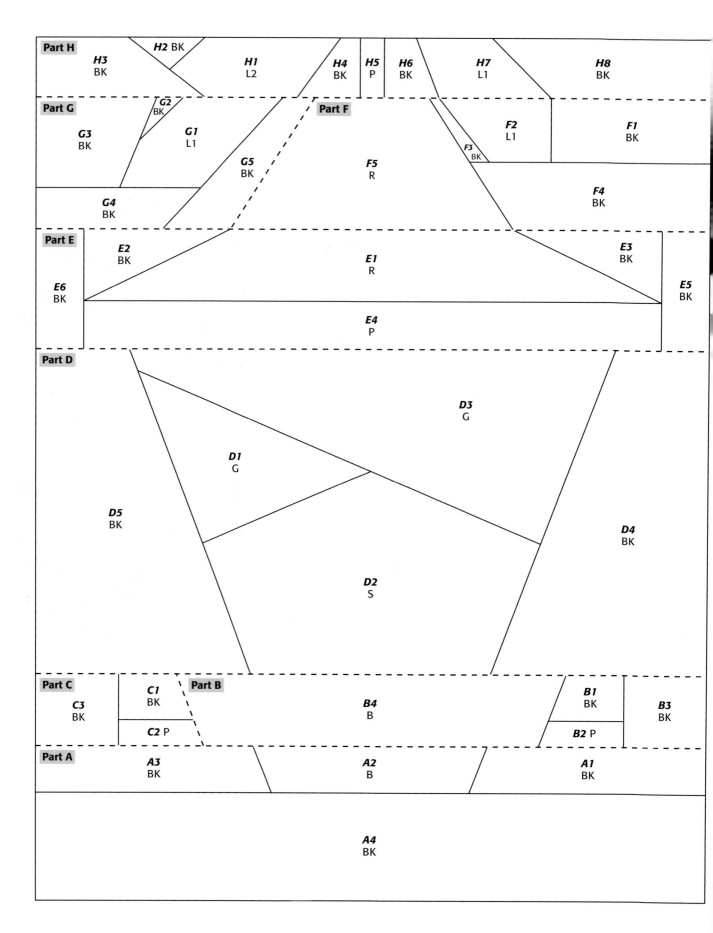

Part H

H3 BK
H2 BK
H1 L2
H4 BK
H5 P
H6 BK
H7 L1
H8 BK

Part G

G2 BK
G3 BK
G1 L1
G5 BK

Part F

F2 L1
F3 BK
F1 BK
F5 R
F4 BK

G4 BK

Part E

E2 BK
E6 BK
E1 R
E3 BK
E5 BK
E4 P

Part D

D3 G
D1 G
D5 BK
D4 BK
D2 S

Part C

C3 BK
C1 BK
Part B
B4 B
B1 BK
B3 BK
C2 P
B2 P

Part A

A3 BK
A2 B
A1 BK
A4 BK

Covered Tray Bird Feeder

Normally this is a large feeder that allows many birds of a wide variety to feed at the same time. It can truly become "standing room only" at mealtimes. Not only does it allow the birds to perch at the edge, but it also allows some in the middle to be a bit more picky about their seed selection and the cracking open of their favorites.

Fabric Key

BK—Background Sky
L1—Leaf 1
L2—Leaf 2
L3—Leaf 3
R—Roof
S—Seed
T—Trim
W—Wood

Sewing Order

Part A: 1–7
Part B: 1–4
Join A to B (AB)
Part C: 1–3
Join AB to C (ABC)
Part D: 1–3
Join ABC to D (ABCD)
Part E: 1–5
Join ABCD to E (ABCDE)
Part F: 1–6
Join ABCDE to F (ABCDEF)
Part G: 1–11
Join ABCDEF to G (ABCDEFG)
Part H: 1–6
Join ABCDEFG to H (ABCDEFGH)
Part I: 1–7
Part J: 1–7
Join I to J (IJ)
Join ABCDEFGH to IJ
　　(ABCDEFGHIJ)

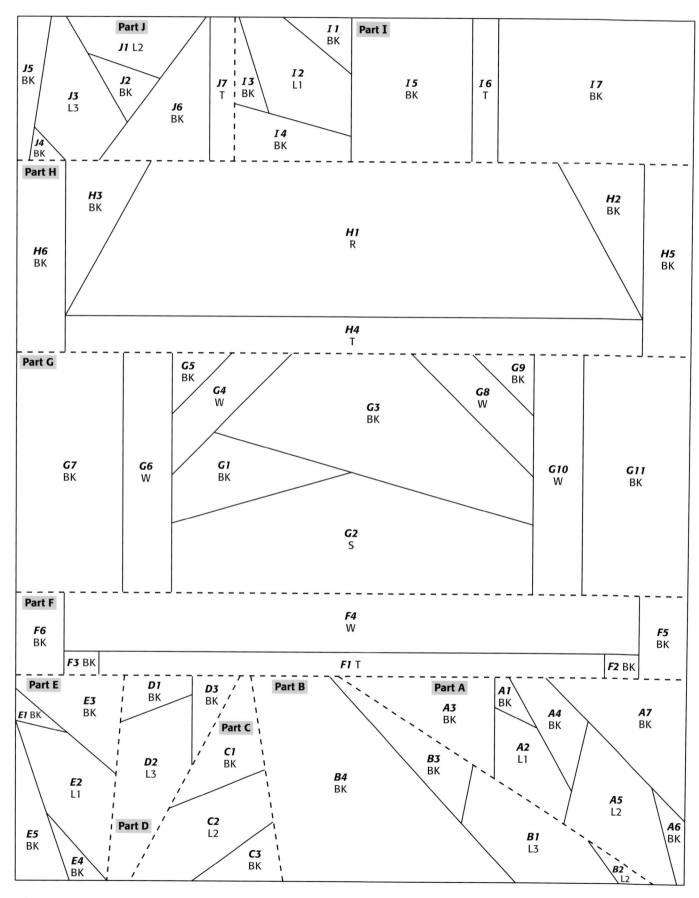

Double-Sided Arbor Bird Feeder

Hang this feeder from a branch and watch it spin and sway as birds land on either side. Their fluttering from side to side causes the feeder to twist and turn. Hang on! Don't get dizzy now!

Fabric Key

BK—Background Sky
L—Leaf
R—Roof
S—Seeds
T—Tree
W—Wood Siding

Sewing Order

Part A: 1–4
Part B: 1–4
Part C: 1–10
Join B to C (BC)
Part D: 1–4
Join BC to D (BCD)
Join A to BCD (ABCD)
Part E: 1–2
Join ABCD to E (ABCDE)
Part F: 1–3
Join ABCDE to F (ABCDEF)
Part G: 1
Join ABCDEF to G (ABCDEFG)
Part H: 1–4
Part I: 1–6
Join H to I (HI)
Join ABCDEFG to HI
   (ABCDEFGHI)

• *I3* BK

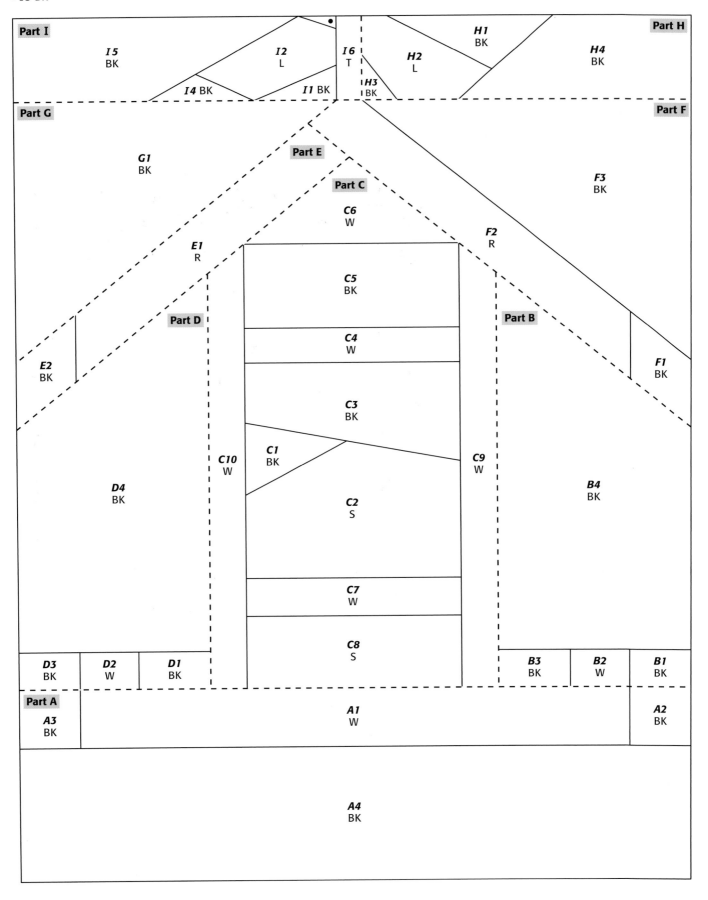

Hummingbird Feeder

W ho can resist enjoying the antics of those tiny humming birds as they dart and weave around this bright red bottle feeder? Their tiny wings become almost invisible as they "pause to refresh" at this feeder. Let this feeder bring a bright flash of color to your quilt tops!

Fabric Key

BK—Background Sky
G—Glass
L—Liquid
R—Red
Y—Yellow

Sewing Order

Part A: 1–6
Part B: 1–3
Join A to B (AB)
Part C: 1–4
Join AB to C (ABC)
Part D: 1–5
Part E: 1–4
Join D to E (DE)
Join ABC to DE (ABCDE)
Part F: 1–7
Join ABCDE to F (ABCDEF)

Block Embellishment

Sew ¾"-diameter flower button where indicated.

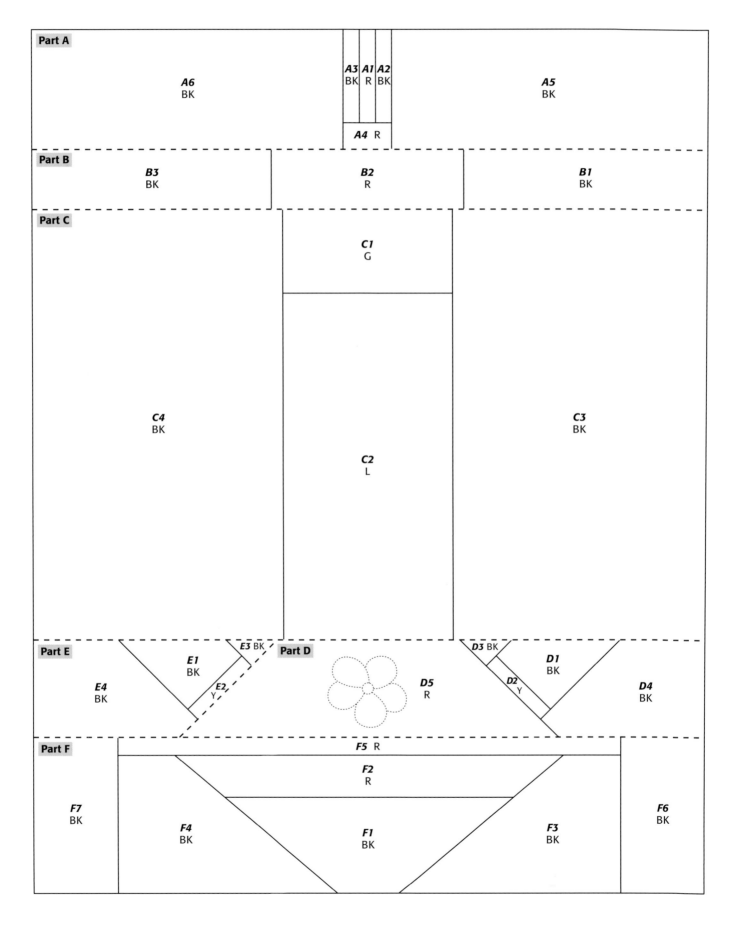

Shed Roof Bird Feeder

The shape of this feeder is what calls to me. I like the overhanging roof that provides some protection to those feeding here. What beauty to see the color and profile of each visitor—the top-notch of the cardinal, the flitting tail of the chickadee, or the bright yellow of the goldfinch. Make this feeder, and just watch the birds enjoy the feast!

Fabric Key

BK—Background Sky
L1—Leaf 1
L2—Leaf 2
L3—Leaf 3
S—Siding
T—Trim
W—Wood

Sewing Order

Part A: 1–7
Part B: 1–10
Join A to B (AB)
Part C: 1–4
Join AB to C (ABC)
Part D: 1–10
Join ABC to D (ABCD)

Part E: 1–3
Part F: 1–5
Join E to F (EF)
Join ABCD to EF (ABCDEF)
Part G: 1–7
Part H: 1–6
Join G to H (GH)
Join ABCDEF to GH (ABCDEFGH)

• **D10** BK

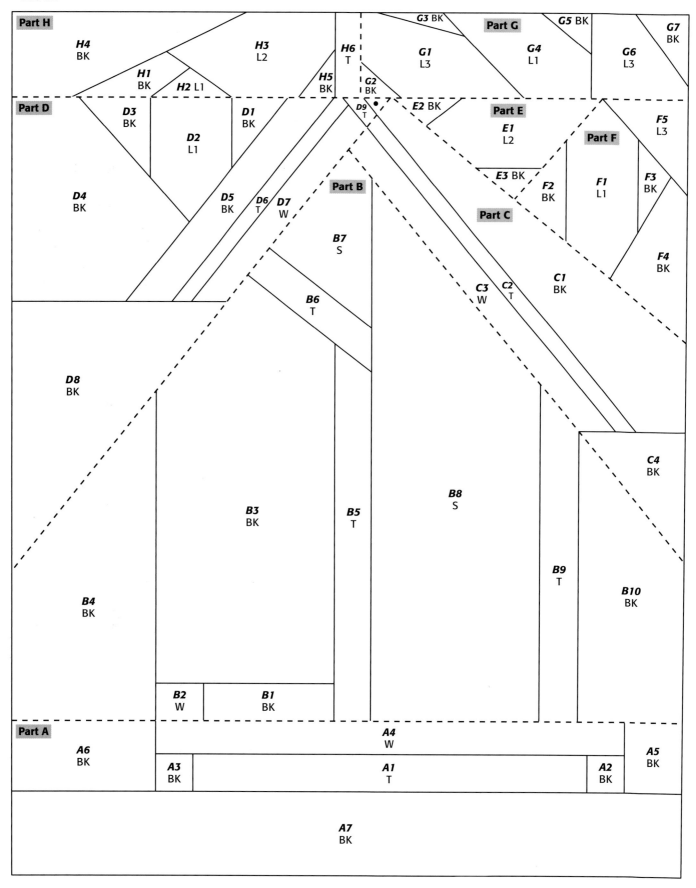

Butterfly House

Their long, narrow slits let the butterflies in but keep danger out, so many gardens are now being graced with the addition of these houses. Can't you just visualize a beautiful butterfly landing softly on the perch, slowly folding back its wings and stepping through the narrow slit to enjoy a quiet rest from its flight, safe and secure?

Fabric Key

B—Black
BK—Background Sky
GR—Ground
L1—Leaf 1
L2—Leaf 2
L3—Leaf 3
P—Pole/Perches
R—Roof
S—Siding
T1—Trim 1
T2—Trim 2

Sewing Order

Section I
Part A: 1–6
Part B: 1–8
Part C: 1–6
Join B to C (BC)
Part D: 1–6
Join BC to D (BCD)

Part E: 1–3
Join BCD to E (BCDE)
Part F: 1–3
Join BCDE to F (BCDEF)
Join A to BCDEF (ABCDEF)
Part G: 1–5
Join ABCDEF to G (ABCDEFG)
Part H: 1–9
Join ABCDEFG to H
   (ABCDEFGH)
Part I: 1–4
Join ABCDEFGH to I
   (ABCDEFGHI)

Section II
Part A: 1
Part B: 1–4
Part C: 1–4
Join B to C (BC)
Part D: 1
Join BC to D (BCD)
Part E: 1

Join BCD to E (BCDE)
Part F: 1–3
Part G: 1–4
Part H: 1–4
Join G to H (GH)
Join F to GH (FGH)
Part I: 1–4
Join FGH to I (FGHI)
Part J: 1
Join FGHI to J (FGHIJ)
Join BCDE to FGHIJ
   (BCDEFGHIJ)
Join A to BCDEFGHIJ
   (ABCDEFGHIJ)
Join Section I to Section II

Block Embellishments

Sew buttons or appliqués to block as desired (refer to "Appliqués" on page 20).

Butterfly House: Section I

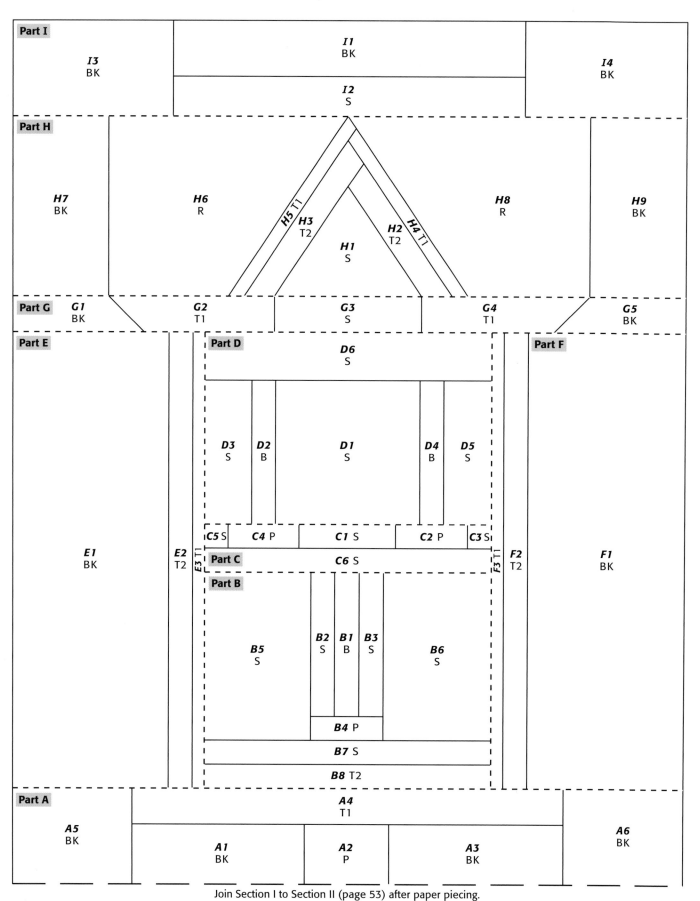

Join Section I to Section II (page 53) after paper piecing.

Butterfly House: Section II

Join Section II to Section I (page 52) after paper piecing.

Part D

Part E

Part J

J1
BK

D1
BK

Part H

G3
GR

G4
GR

H4
GR

E1
P

G2
GR

Part G

C3
GR

C4
GR

H3
GR

Part C

C2
GR

Part B

Part I

B4
GR

G1
L2

I4
GR

C1
L1

H1
L1

F2
GR

B3
GR

B1
L2

I2
GR

H2
GR

Part F

F1
L3

I1
L3

B2
GR

I3
GR

Part A

F3
GR

A1
GR

Finch Feeder

Those tiny black seeds call to an entirely different set of birds—in fact, multitudes of them! What great joy it is to see all the perches full, with even more birds flitting close by demanding their turn to partake of those special finch seeds.

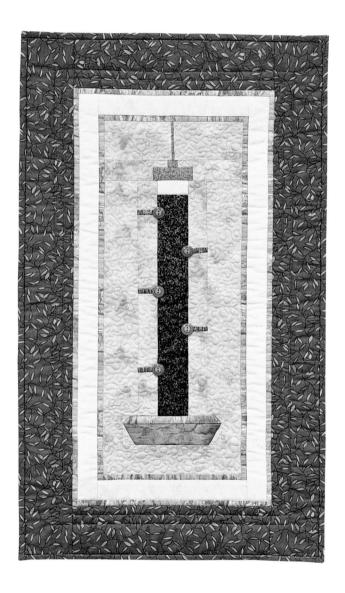

Fabric Key

BK—Background Sky
DB—Dark Base
G—Glass
LB—Light Base
P—Perch
S—Seed
T—Trim

Sewing Order

Part A: 1–3
Part B: 1–6
Join A to B (AB)
Part C: 1–8
Part D: 1–2
Join C to D (CD)

Part E: 1–6
Join CD to E (CDE)
Join AB to CDE
 (ABCDE)
Part F: 1–9
Join ABCDE to F
 (ABCDEF)

Block Embellishments

Sew 1/2"-diameter button to each perch where indicated.

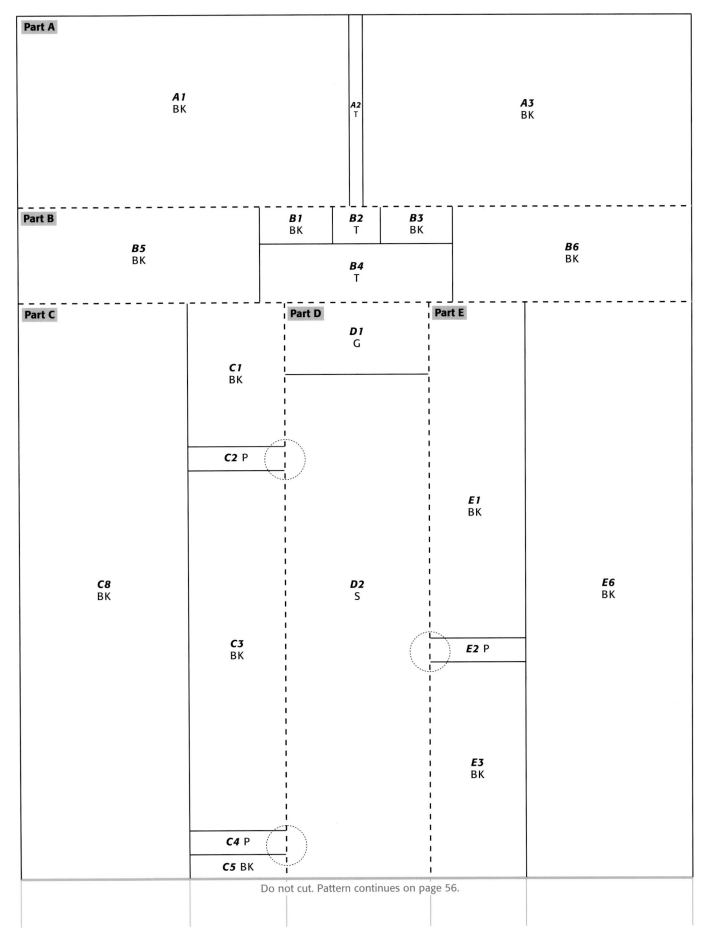

Do not cut. Pattern continues on page 56.

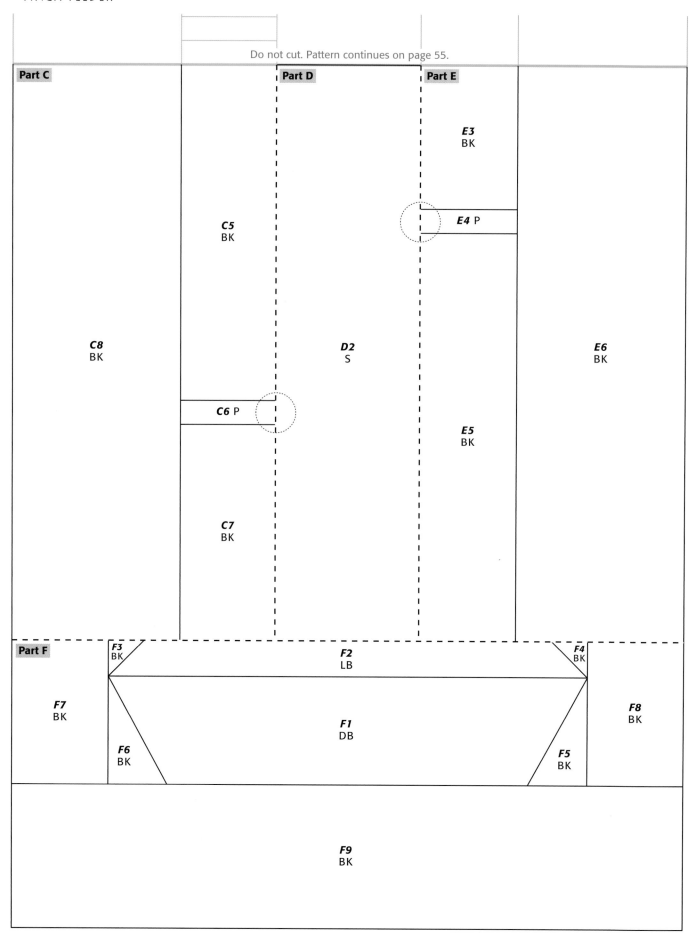

Do not cut. Pattern continues on page 55.

Part C

Part D

Part E

E3
BK

C5
BK

E4 P

C8
BK

D2
S

E6
BK

C6 P

E5
BK

C7
BK

Part F

F3
BK

F2
LB

F4
BK

F7
BK

F8
BK

F1
DB

F6
BK

F5
BK

F9
BK

Pole Birdhouse

F or those birds who enjoy a home more out in the open and closer to the ground, build this house and watch the fun as the occupants fly back and forth carrying nest-building materials and feeding their babies. My husband and I were once fortunate enough to have a family of bluebirds occupy our pole birdhouse. What a glorious gift! Maybe your house will attract a pair, too.

Fabric Key

BK—Background Sky
G—Grass/Ground
L1—Leaf 1
L2—Leaf 2
L3—Leaf 3
P—Pole/Post
T—Tin
W1—Wood 1
W2—Wood 2
W3—Wood 3

Sewing Order

Section I
Part A: 1–20
Part B: 1–3
Join A to B (AB)

Section II
Part A: 1
Part B: 1–4
Part C: 1–4
Join B to C (BC)
Part D: 1
Join BC to D (BCD)
Part E: 1
Join BCD to E (BCDE)
Part F: 1–3
Part G: 1–4
Part H: 1–4
Join G to H (GH)
Join F to GH (FGH)
Part I: 1–4
Join FGH to I (FGHI)

Part J: 1
Join FGHI to J (FGHIJ)
Join BCDE to FGHIJ
    (BCDEFGHIJ)
Join A to BCDEFGHIJ
    (ABCDEFGHIJ)
Join Section I to Section II

Block Embellishments

• Sew 7/8"-diameter button where indicated for bird entry hole.
• Sew 4 seed beads around entry hole section where indicated for nail heads.

Pole Birdhouse: Section I

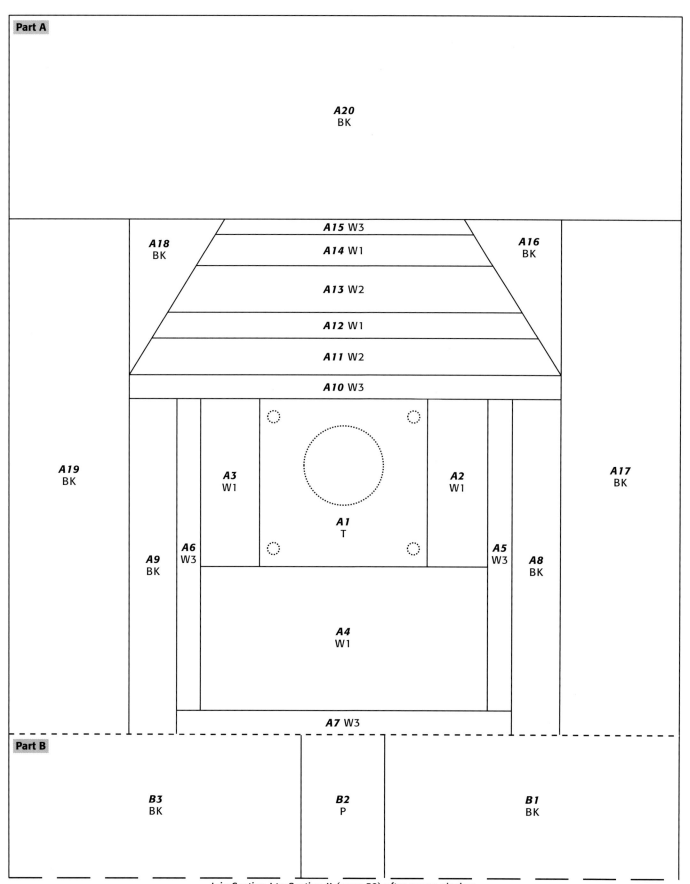

Join Section I to Section II (page 59) after paper piecing.

Pole Birdhouse: Section II
Join Section II to Section I (page 58) after paper piecing.

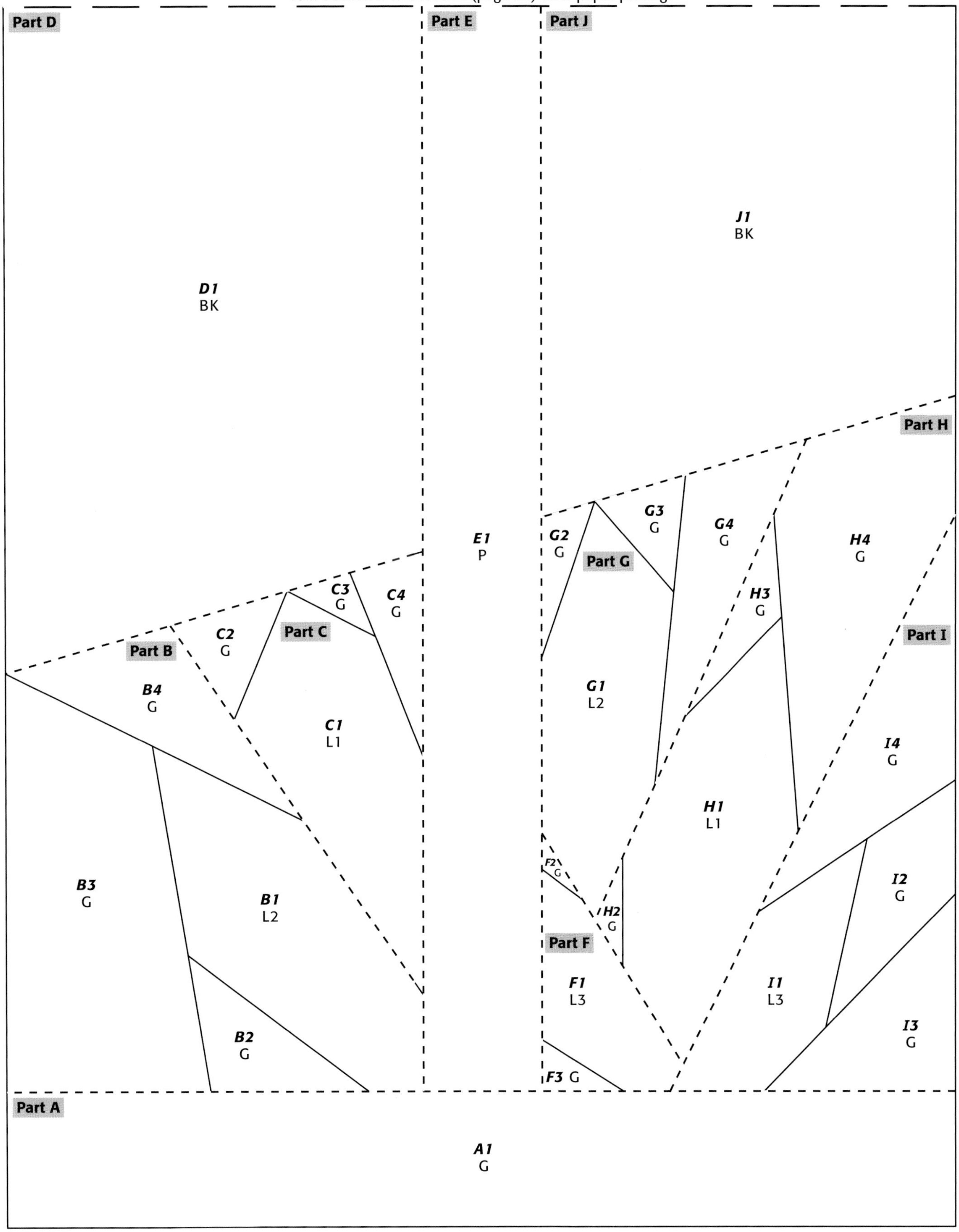

Part D

Part E

Part J

J1
BK

D1
BK

Part H

E1
P

G3
G

G4
G

H4
G

G2
G

Part G

H3
G

C3
G

C4
G

Part C

Part I

C2
G

Part B

B4
G

G1
L2

I4
G

C1
L1

H1
L1

B3
G

B1
L2

F2
G

I2
G

H2
G

Part F

B2
G

F1
L3

I1
L3

I3
G

F3 G

Part A

A1
G

Two-Story Birdhouse

T wice the height, twice the fun! Build this two-story bird-house and call for more than one family of birds. It's twice as tall as the other houses but lets you show off twice as much of some wonderful fabric. Double occupancy allows for double the fun!

Fabric Key

A—Accent
B—Branch
BK—Background Sky
L1—Leaf 1
L2—Leaf 2
L3—Leaf 3
R—Roof
S1—Siding 1
S2—Siding 2
T—Trim

Sewing Order

Section I
Part A: 1–11
Part B: 1–6
Join A to B (AB)
Part C: 1–5
Part D: 1–4
Join C to D (CD)
Part E: 1
Join CD to E (CDE)
Part F: 1–3
Part G: 1–5
Join F to G (FG)
Part H: 1–3
Join FG to H (FGH)
Join CDE to FGH (CDEFGH)
Join AB to CDEFGH (ABCDEFGH)

Section II
Part A: 1–5
Part B: 1–3
Join A to B (AB)
Part C: 1–5
Part D: 1–3
Join C to D (CD)

Join AB to CD (ABCD)
Join Section I to Section II

Section III
Part A: 1–4
Part B: 1–8
Join A to B (AB)
Part C: 1–9
Join AB to C (ABC)
Join Sections I and II to Section III

Block Embellishments

- Sew $7/8$"-diameter buttons where indicated for bird entry holes.
- Sew $3/8$"-diameter buttons where indicated for perch.

60

Two-Story Birdhouse: Section I

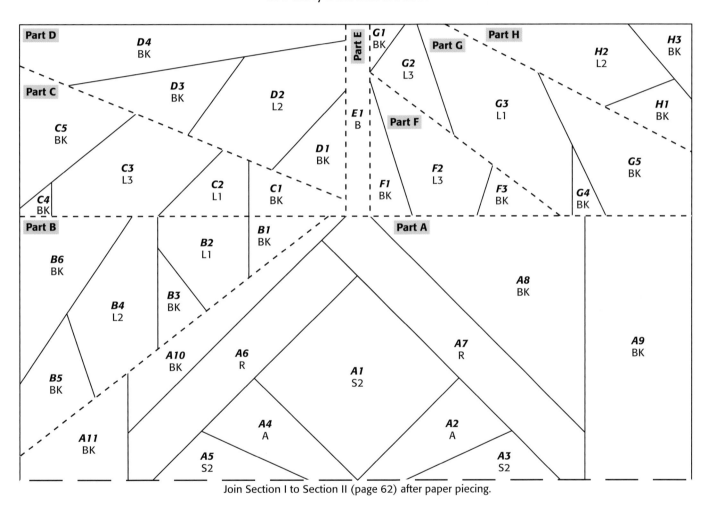

Join Section I to Section II (page 62) after paper piecing.

Two-Story Birdhouse: Section II

Join Section II to Section I (page 61) after paper piecing.

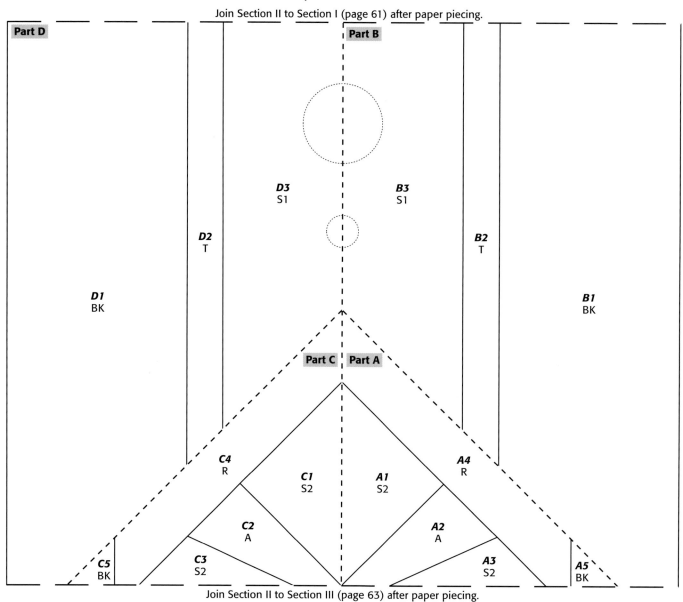

Join Section II to Section III (page 63) after paper piecing.

Two-Story Birdhouse: Section III

Join Section III to Section II (page 62) after paper piecing.

Part C

C9
BK

C8
T

C7
S1

C1
S1

C4
S1

C5
T

C6
BK

C2 A

C3
S1

Part B

B3
BK

B1
A

B2
BK

B7
BK

B8
BK

B4
T

B6
BK

B5
BK

Part A

A2 A

A4
BK

A1
BK

A3
BK

Blossoms

irds and flowers go hand in hand. Use either or both of these blossoms in your quilts as corner blocks or as corner posts with sashing. Paint them in coordinating colors to emphasize a theme or splash them with high contrasting colors for fun and surprise. If only the real blossoms in our gardens would last so long and so well!

4-Petal Blossom

Fabric Key

BK—Background
C—Center
F—Flower Petals

Join A to B (AB)
Part C: 1–5
Part D: 1–5
Join C to D (CD)
Join AB to CD (ABCD)

Sewing Order

Part A: 1–6
Part B: 1–5

5-Petal Blossom

Fabric Key

BK—Background
C—Center
F—Flower Petals

Join A to B (AB)
Part C: 1–4
Part D: 1–5
Join C to D (CD)
Part E: 1–5
Join CD to E (CDE)
Join AB to CDE
   (ABCDE)

Sewing Order

Part A: 1–5
Part B: 1–5

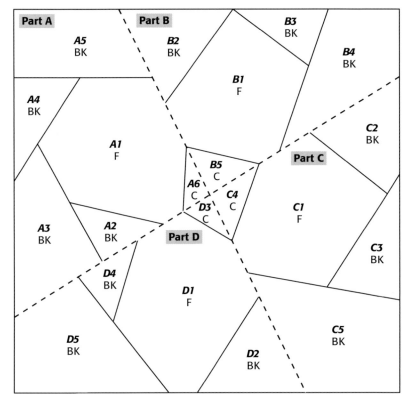

4-Petal Blossom

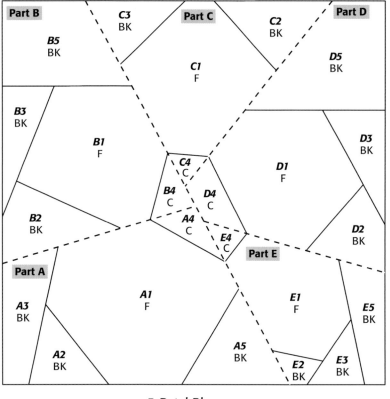

5-Petal Blossom

Bluebird

Married for more than fifty years, my grandparents, Velma and Edgar Parker, always loved bluebirds. When they corresponded with each other they always signed off, "Love from your Bluebird Pal." This small 4" x 4" block is dedicated to them and is designed to exemplify the phrase, "Bluebirds of Happiness." Let its flash of bright color and saucy shape grace the corners of your quilts with a cheerful note or use it as the corner posts within the central part of your work (see "Fly Away Home" on page 84).

Fabric Key

BK—Background Sky
F—Feathers
W1—Wing 1
W2—Wing 2

Sewing Order

Part A: 1–4
Part B: 1–8
Join A to B (AB)
Part C: 1–3
Part D: 1–6
Join C to D (CD)
Join AB to CD (ABCD)

Block Embellishment

Sew seed bead where indicated for eye.

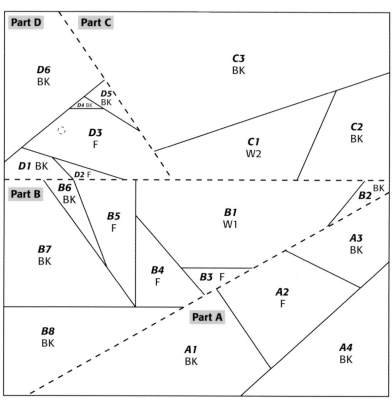

Chickadee

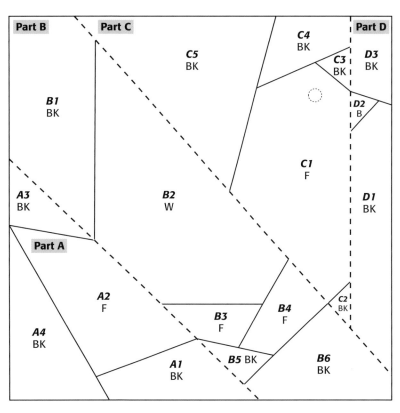

This little bird is just plain cute. He's plump and full of cheer. Add him to your quilts and bring a touch of whimsy to your houses and feeders.

Fabric Key

B—Beak
BK—Background
F—Feathers
W—Wing

Sewing Order

Part A: 1–4
Part B: 1–6
Join A to B (AB)
Part C: 1–5
Part D: 1–3
Join C to D (CD)
Join AB to CD (ABCD)

Block Embellishment

Sew seed bead where indicated for eye.

Dove

With wings fluttering and tail feathers spread out, this dove in flight is looking for a place to land. Why not build a selection of birdhouses and let her pick her favorite?

Fabric Key

B—Beak
BK—Background
DF—Dark Feathers
F—Feathers

Sewing Order

Part A: 1–8
Part B: 1–6
Part C: 1–2
Join B to C (BC)
Part D: 1–7
Join BC to D (BCD)
Join A to BCD (ABCD)

Block Embellishment

Sew seed bead where indicated for eye.

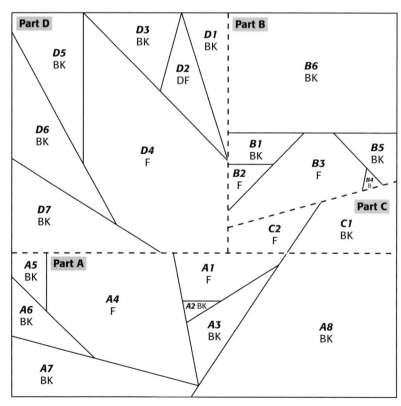

Branch

This branch magically grows from 4½" x 17" to 4½" x 34" when you add a mirror-image block to the one shown below (see "Trace the Pattern onto the Foundation" on page 9).

Fabric Key

BK—Background
BR—Branch
L1—Leaf 1 (light green)
L2—Leaf 2 (medium-light green)
L3—Leaf 3 (medium-dark green)
L4—Leaf 4 (dark green)

Sewing Order

Section I

Part A: 1–5
Part B: 1–3
Join A to B (AB)
Part C: 1–3
Join AB to C (ABC)
Part D: 1–5
Join ABC to D (ABCD)
Part E: 1
Join ABCD to E (ABCDE)
Part F: 1–5

Part G: 1–6
Join F to G (FG)
Join ABCDE to FG (ABCDEFG)

Section II

Part A: 1–4
Part B: 1–4
Join A to B (AB)
Part C: 1–8
Join AB to C (ABC)
Part D: 1–6
Join ABC to D (ABCD)
Part E: 1
Join ABCD to E (ABCDE)
Part F: 1–5
Part G: 1–4
Join F to G (FG)
Part H: 1–6
Join FG to H (FGH)
Part I: 1–7
Join FGH to I (FGHI)

Join ABCDE to FGHI
   (ABCDEFGHI)
Join Section I to Section II

Section III

Part A: 1–6
Part B: 1–3
Join A to B (AB)
Part C: 1–3
Join AB to C (ABC)
Part D: 1–4
Part E: 1–5
Join D to E (DE)
Join ABC to DE (ABCDE)
Join Sections I and II to
   Section III

Block Embellishment

Sew on lots of buttons in all different sizes to represent berries or blossoms on the branch.

Branch: Section I

Join Section I to Section II (page 71) after paper piecing.

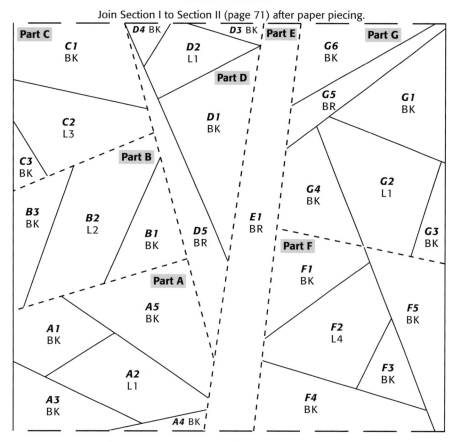

Join to a mirror-image branch block after paper piecing.

Branch: Section III

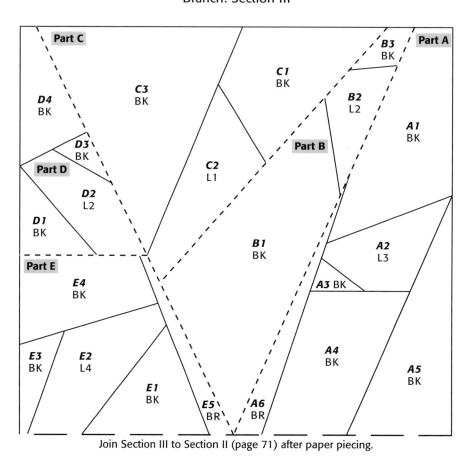

Join Section III to Section II (page 71) after paper piecing.

Branch: Section II

Join Section II to Section III (page 70) after paper piecing.

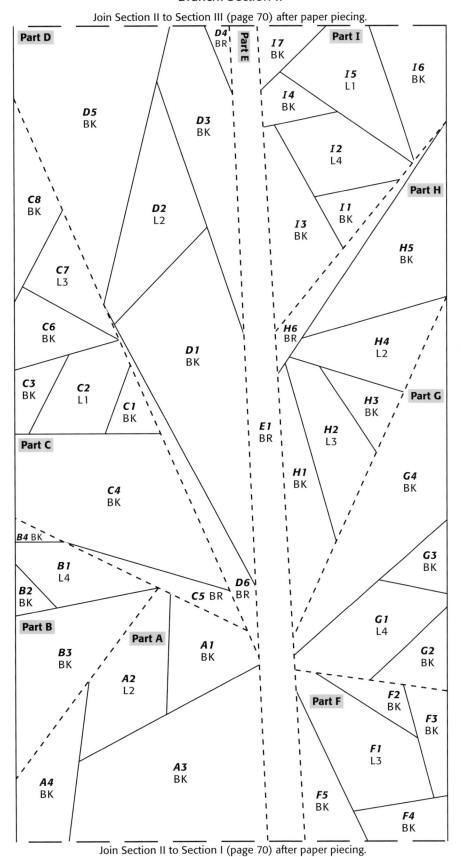

Part D

Part E

D4
BR

I7
BK

Part I

I5
L1

I6
BK

D5
BK

D3
BK

I4
BK

I2
L4

C8
BK

D2
L2

Part H

I1
BK

I3
BK

H5
BK

C7
L3

C6
BK

D1
BK

H6
BR

H4
L2

C3
BK

C2
L1

C1
BK

Part G

H3
BK

Part C

E1
BR

H2
L3

H1
BK

G4
BK

C4
BK

B4 BK

B1
L4

G3
BK

B2
BK

Part B

D6
BR

C5 BR

G1
L4

Part A

A1
BK

G2
BK

B3
BK

A2
L2

Part F

F2
BK

F3
BK

F1
L3

A4
BK

A3
BK

F5
BK

F4
BK

Join Section II to Section I (page 70) after paper piecing.

Individual-Block Wall Hangings

The small quilts featured in this book are just the right size for gift giving or for those small areas of your home that need a bit of color and cheer. Two sizes are presented: 15" x 17" finished wall hangings are constructed using the 7" x 9" blocks, and longer 15" x 26" wall hangings feature 7" x 18" blocks. Each quilt is framed with four borders, two of which are $\frac{1}{4}$"-wide framing borders.

WALL HANGINGS FOR 7" X 9" BLOCKS

Finished Wall Hanging Size: 15" x 17"

Materials: 42"-wide fabric

12" x 14" rectangle for block background
Assorted scraps for house or feeder (refer to individual pattern)
$\frac{1}{8}$ yd. or scrap for accent borders
$\frac{1}{8}$ yd. or scrap for inner border
$\frac{3}{8}$ yd. for outer border and binding
$\frac{3}{4}$ yd. for backing
20" x 22" piece of batting
Buttons or scraps of fabrics for appliqués of entry holes and perches, if needed

Cutting

After cutting the following pieces, use the remaining fabrics in the block.

From the accent border fabric, cut:

2 strips, each $\frac{3}{4}$" x 42". Crosscut to make:
    2 strips, each $\frac{3}{4}$" x $7\frac{1}{2}$", for inner top and bottom accent borders
    4 strips, each $\frac{3}{4}$" x 10", for inner side accent borders and outer top and bottom accent borders

2 strips, each $\frac{3}{4}$" x $12\frac{1}{2}$", for outer side accent borders

From the inner border fabric, cut:

1 strip, $1\frac{1}{2}$" x 42". Crosscut to make:
    2 strips, each $1\frac{1}{2}$" x 8", for inner top and bottom borders
    2 strips, each $1\frac{1}{2}$" x 12", for inner side borders

From the outer border and binding fabric, cut:

2 strips, each 2" x 42", for binding
2 strips, each 3" x 42". Crosscut to make:
    2 strips, each 3" x $10\frac{1}{2}$", for outer top and bottom borders
    2 strips, each 3" x $17\frac{1}{2}$", for outer side borders

From the backing and rod pocket fabric, cut:

1 piece, 20" x 22", for backing

Assembly

1. Trace the 7" x 9" foundation pattern for the desired birdhouse or bird feeder onto freezer paper.
2. Refer to "Steps to Successful Paper Foundation Piecing" (pages 9–15) to construct the block, following the Sewing Order and Fabric Key for the desired block (pages 25–49). Each block should measure $7\frac{1}{2}$" x $9\frac{1}{2}$" before adding any borders. If it does not, be sure to adjust the length of the border strips accordingly.
3. Refer to "Framing Your Projects" (pages 15–18) for directions on applying the inner accent border, then the inner border. Repeat to apply the outer accent border and outer border.

Finishing

Refer to "Fine Finishes" on pages 19–24.

1. Embroider and appliqué any desired block details.

2. Layer the quilt top with batting and backing; baste.

3. Quilt as desired, or stitch in the ditch around each part of the birdhouse or feeder and then along each separate border. The background area of each structure may be stipple quilted or left unquilted. In the outer border, add two additional rows of parallel stitching approximately $1/2$" and 1" from the seam line.

4. Square up the quilt top.

5. Add a rod pocket and bind the quilt.

6. Add desired bead or button embellishments.

7. Stitch a label to the quilt back.

WALL HANGINGS FOR 7" X 18" BLOCKS

Finished Wall Hanging Size: 15" x 26"

Materials: 42"-wide fabric

9" x 42" for block background

Assorted scraps for the structure (refer to individual pattern)

$1/4$ yd. for accent borders

$1/4$ yd. for inner border

$3/8$ yd. for outer border and binding

$3/4$ yd. for backing

20" x 30" square of batting

Buttons or scraps of fabrics for appliqués for entry holes and perches, if needed

Cutting

After cutting the following pieces, use the remaining fabrics in the block.

From the accent border fabric, cut:

3 strips, each $3/4$" x 42". Crosscut to make:
    2 strips, each $3/4$" x $7^1/2$", for inner top and bottom accent borders
    2 strips, each $3/4$" x 19", for inner side accent borders
    2 strips, each $3/4$" x 10", for outer top and bottom accent borders
    2 strips, each $3/4$" x $21^1/2$", for outer side accent borders

From the inner border fabric, cut:

2 strips, each $1^1/2$" x 42". Crosscut to make:
    2 strips, each $1^1/2$" x 8", for inner top and bottom borders
    2 strips, each $1^1/2$" x 21", for inner side borders

From the outer border and binding fabric, cut:

2 strips, each 2" x 42", for binding

2 strips, each 3" x 42". Crosscut to make:
    2 strips, each 3" x $10^1/2$", for outer top and bottom borders
    2 strips, each 3" x $26^1/2$", for outer side borders

From the backing fabric, cut:

1 piece, 20" x 30", for backing

Assembly

1. Trace the 7" x 18" foundation pattern for the desired house or feeder onto freezer paper.

2. Refer to "Steps to Successful Paper Foundation Piecing" (pages 9–15) to construct the block, following the Sewing Order and Fabric Key for the desired block (pages 51–60). Each block should measure $7^1/2$" x $18^1/2$" before adding any borders. If it does not, be sure to adjust the length of the border strips accordingly.

3. Refer to "Framing Your Projects" (pages 15–18) for directions on applying the inner accent border, then the inner border. Repeat to apply the outer accent border and outer border.

Finishing

Refer to "Fine Finishes" on pages 19–24.

1. Embroider and appliqué any desired block details.

2. Layer the quilt top with batting and backing; baste.

3. Quilt as desired, or stitch in the ditch around each part of the birdhouse or feeder and then along each separate border. The background area of each structure may be stipple quilted or left unquilted. In the outer border, add two additional rows of parallel stitching approximately $1/2$" and 1" from the seam line.

4. Square up the quilt top.

5. Add a rod pocket and bind the quilt.

6. Add desired bead or button embellishments.

7. Stitch a label to the quilt back.

All around the Neighborhood

Open up that stash of fabric and create your own parade of homes with this large sampler quilt. Begin by choosing twelve of the 7" x 9" house and feeder blocks and four of the 7" x 18" blocks. Surround each block with multiple borders in a variety of colors, and then sash them with a green leaf print and brown corner posts. Finish it up by encircling the blocks with a wide border of flying birds, and you can well appreciate this quilt's title of "All around the Neighborhood."

Finished size: 74" x 91"

Materials: 42"-wide fabric

$2\frac{1}{2}$ yds. for block backgrounds

Assorted scraps for the birdhouse and feeder structures, and the leaves and branches

$\frac{1}{8}$ yd. *each* of 16 assorted fabrics for block accent borders

$\frac{1}{4}$ yd. *each* of 16 assorted fabrics for block inner borders

$\frac{1}{4}$ yd. *each* of 16 assorted fabrics for block outer borders

$1\frac{3}{8}$ yds. for sashing

$\frac{3}{4}$ yd. for corner posts and binding

$\frac{3}{8}$ yd. for quilt inner border

3 yds. for quilt outer border

6 yds. for backing

78" x 96" piece of batting

Assorted buttons or appliqué fabrics for entry holes and perches

Cutting

After cutting the following pieces, use the remaining fabrics in the blocks.

From each of the 16 assorted block accent border fabrics, cut:

3 strips, each $\frac{3}{4}$" x 42"

From each of the 16 assorted block inner border fabrics, cut:

2 strips, each $1\frac{1}{2}$" x 42"

From each of the 16 assorted block outer border fabrics, cut:

2 strips, each 3" x 42"

From the sashing fabric, cut:

17 strips, each $2\frac{1}{2}$" x 42". Crosscut to make:

    20 strips, each $2\frac{1}{2}$" x $13\frac{1}{2}$", for horizontal sashing

    17 strips, each $2\frac{1}{2}$" x $15\frac{1}{2}$", for vertical sashing for 7" x 9" blocks

    3 strips, each $2\frac{1}{2}$" x $24\frac{1}{2}$", for vertical sashing for 7" x 18" blocks

    2 strips, each $2\frac{1}{2}$" x $7\frac{1}{2}$", for short vertical sashing units

From the corner post and binding fabric, cut:

2 strips, each $2\frac{1}{2}$" x 42". Crosscut to make 27 squares, each $2\frac{1}{2}$" x $2\frac{1}{2}$", for corner posts.

8 strips, each 2" x 42", for binding

From the quilt inner border fabric, cut:

8 strips, each $1\frac{1}{2}$" x 42"

From the quilt outer border fabric, cut:

2 strips, each $5\frac{1}{2}$" x 80", along the lengthwise grain for the outer top and bottom borders

2 strips, each $5\frac{1}{2}$" x 96", along the lengthwise grain for the outer side borders

From the backing fabric, cut:

2 pieces, each 42" x 97"

Assembly

1. Using the 7" x 9" foundation patterns for the birdhouse and bird feeder blocks on pages 25–49, trace 1 each of 12 patterns. Trace 1 each of the four 7" x 18" blocks (pages 51–60).

2. Refer to "Steps to Successful Paper Foundation Piecing" (pages 9–15) to construct the 16 houses and bird feeders, following the Sewing Order and Fabric Key for each individual block (pages 25–60).

3. Refer to "Framing Your Projects" (pages 15–18) for directions on applying the block inner accent border, then the block inner border to each block. Repeat to apply the block outer accent border and block outer border to each block. With borders, the smaller blocks should measure $15\frac{1}{2}$" x $17\frac{1}{2}$" and the larger blocks should measure $15\frac{1}{2}$" x $26\frac{1}{2}$".

4. Leaving approximately 2" of outer border on each side, use your rotary cutting equipment to trim the 12 smaller blocks to $13\frac{1}{2}$" x $15\frac{1}{2}$"; trim the 4 larger blocks to $13\frac{1}{2}$" x $24\frac{1}{2}$". Be sure the block is centered before cutting.

NOTE: Trimming the blocks ensures that all of the blocks will finish to the same size so the sashing strips and corner posts will fit correctly.

5. Arrange the birdhouse, butterfly house, and bird feeder blocks as shown.

6. Make 2 horizontal block rows. To make each row, alternately stitch together 5 vertical sashing strips and 4 smaller blocks, beginning and ending with a sashing strip. Press the seam allowances toward the sashing strips.

2½" x 15½"

7. Make 2 inner and 2 outer vertical block rows. To make each row, alternately stitch together 1 small block and 1 large block with a horizontal sashing strip as shown. Press the seam allowances toward the sashing strips.

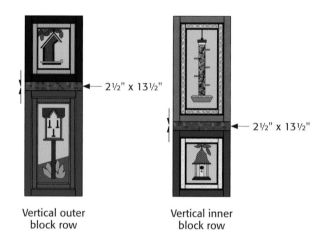

Vertical outer
block row

Vertical inner
block row

8. Make 4 horizontal sashing rows. To make each row, alternately sew together 5 corner posts and 4 horizontal sashing strips, beginning and ending with a corner post. Press the seam allowances toward the sashing strips.

2½" x 13½"   2½" x 2½"

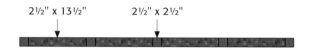

9. Make 5 vertical sashing rows. To make the rows, alternately stitch together the vertical sashing strips and corner posts as shown. Press the seam allowances toward the sashing strips.

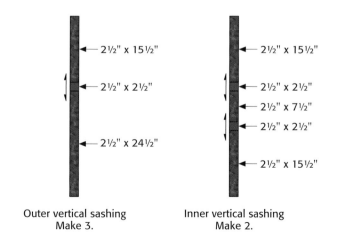

Outer vertical sashing
Make 3.

Inner vertical sashing
Make 2.

10. Assemble the horizontal sashing and block rows as shown. Stitch the rows together. Press the seam allowances toward the sashing rows.

11. Assemble the vertical sashing and block rows as shown. Stitch the rows together. Press the seam allowances toward the sashing rows. Stitch the remaining horizontal sashing row to the bottom of the vertical rows. Press the seam allowance toward the sashing row.

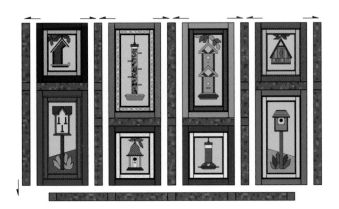

12. Stitch the horizontal and vertical rows together. Press the seam allowance toward the horizontal sashing row.

13. Stitch 2 quilt inner border strips together end to end to make one long strip for the side borders. Make 4. Stitch a side border strip to each side of the quilt; trim the strips even with the top and bottom edges. Press the seam allowances toward the border strip. Stitch the remaining 2 strips to the top and bottom edges; trim the strips even with the sides. Press the seam allowances toward the border strips.

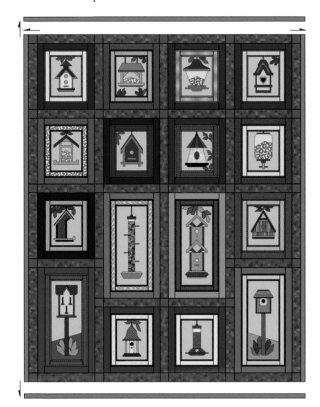

14. Measure the quilt top for borders as described in "Making Borders with Mitered Corners" (page 18). Cut the outer border strips to fit and stitch them to the quilt top, mitering the corners. Press the seam allowance toward the border strips.

Finishing

Refer to "Fine Finishes" on pages 19–24.

1. Embroider and appliqué any desired block details.
2. Stitch the backing pieces together along the long edges to make 1 piece, 84" x 97".
3. Layer the quilt top with batting and the pieced backing; baste.
4. Quilt as desired.
5. Square up the quilt top.
6. Add a rod pocket and bind the quilt.
7. Add any desired bead or button embellishments.
8. Stitch a label to the quilt back.

At Home in the Rose Garden

Let your selection of a beautiful floral print be the inspiration to create this glorious garden retreat. Choose any combination of eighteen 7" x 9" houses and feeders, and arrange them with the alternate Hourglass blocks. Separate each with a gridwork of leafy green sashing and corner posts, and you have created a wonderful habitat for the birds. The background triangles of the Hourglass blocks provide a perfect place to display your embroidery work or fine quilting. Embroider a variety of leaves and allow them to drift across your quilt. Grace each corner with a few tiny fussy-cut or embroidered birds, and truly this quilt will encourage a peaceful, restful feeling as you gaze upon its fabrics, colors, and structures. You, too, can be "At Home in the Rose Garden."

Finished size: 68" x 100"

Materials: 42"-wide fabric

$3\frac{1}{4}$ yds. for foundation block backgrounds and Hourglass block top and bottom triangles*

$\frac{1}{8}$ yd. each or scraps of 15 to 20 assorted fabrics for birdhouse and feeder structures, leaves, and branches

$1\frac{1}{2}$ yds. for sashing

$\frac{3}{8}$ yd. for sashing corner posts

$\frac{5}{8}$ yd. for inner border

1 yd. for middle border

3 yds. for outer border and Hourglass side triangles

6 yds. for backing

74" x 106" piece of batting

$\frac{5}{8}$ yd. for binding

Assorted buttons and/or appliqué fabrics for entry holes and perches

*If you embroider the Hourglass blocks, you will need an additional $1\frac{1}{2}$ yards of fabric to allow for cutting the blocks large enough to hoop.

Cutting

After cutting the following pieces, use the remaining fabrics in the blocks.

From the block background fabric, cut:

5 strips, each $5\frac{1}{4}$" x 42", for Template A triangles*

1 strip, $3\frac{1}{2}$" x 42". Crosscut to make 4 squares, each $3\frac{1}{2}$" x $3\frac{1}{2}$", for middle border corner posts.

From the sashing fabric, cut:

19 strips, each $2\frac{1}{2}$" x 42". Crosscut to make:

40 strips, each $2\frac{1}{2}$" x $7\frac{1}{2}$", for horizontal sashing

42 strips, each $2\frac{1}{2}$" x $9\frac{1}{2}$", for vertical sashing

From the sashing corner post fabric, cut:

3 strips, each $2\frac{1}{2}$" x 42". Crosscut to make 48 squares, each $2\frac{1}{2}$" x $2\frac{1}{2}$".

From the inner border fabric, cut:

8 strips, each $2\frac{1}{4}$" x 42"

From the middle border fabric, cut:

8 strips, each $3\frac{1}{2}$" x 42"

From the outer border fabric, cut:

4 strips, each $6\frac{1}{2}$" x 99", along lengthwise grain for outer borders

3 strips, each $4\frac{1}{4}$" x 99", along lengthwise grain for Template B triangles

From the backing fabric, cut:

2 pieces, each 42" x 108"

From the binding fabric, cut:

9 strips, each 2" x 42"

If you are embroidering the Template A triangles, cut 9 strips, each 9" x 42". Crosscut into 34 rectangles, each 9" x 10".

Assembly

1. Using the 7" x 9" foundation patterns for the birdhouse and feeder blocks on pages 25–49, trace a total of 18 patterns of your choice.
2. Refer to "Steps to Successful Paper Foundation Piecing" (pages 9–15) to construct the blocks, following the Sewing Order and Fabric Keys for each individual block (pages 25–49).

3. *If you have chosen not to include embroidered motifs* in your Hourglass blocks, lay Template A (page 83) on the 5¼" x 42" strip and cut out 34 triangles, alternating the triangle direction with each cut. Repeat to cut 34 triangles using Template B (page 83) and the 4¼" x 99" strips.

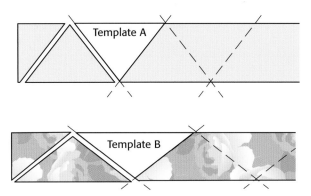

4. Sew an A and B triangle together as shown. Press the seam allowance toward the Template B triangle. Make 34. Stitch 2 AB units together to make the Hourglass block. Press the seam allowance in one direction. Make 17. Each block should measure 7½" x 9½".

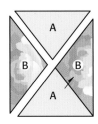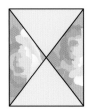

5. *If you have chosen to include embroidered motifs* in your Hourglass blocks, lightly trace Template A onto the 9" x 10" rectangle, positioning the shape so the hoop does not cover the portion that will be embroidered. Follow the embroidery machine manufacturer's instructions to hoop the fabric and embroider the design. Cut out the embroidered triangle. Refer to steps 3 and 4 to cut the Template B triangles and assemble the Hourglass blocks.

MACHINE EMBROIDERY

The machine embroidery on the Hourglass blocks was done on a Husqvarna Viking Designer I sewing/embroidery machine using disks #711 210900 (Birds), #711 222700 (Leaves), and #711 069100 (Diamond Collection 1).

6. To make block rows #1, 3, 5, and 7, alternately stitch together 6 vertical sashing strips, 3 foundation-pieced blocks, and 2 Hourglass blocks as shown. Press the seam allowances toward the sashing. Make 4. To make block rows #2, 4, and 6, alternately stitch together 6 vertical sashing strips, 3 Hourglass blocks, and 2 foundation-pieced blocks as shown. Press the seam allowances toward the sashing. Make 3.

Block rows 1, 3, 5, and 7

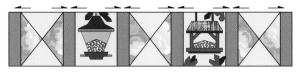

Block rows 2, 4, and 6

7. To make the sashing rows, alternately sew together 6 corner posts and 5 horizontal sashing strips, beginning and ending with a corner post. Press the seam allowances toward the sashing strips. Make 8.

8. Arrange the block rows in numerical order. Alternating sashing and block rows, stitch the rows together, beginning and ending with a sashing row.

9. Stitch 2 inner border strips together end to end to make one long strip. Make 4. Measure the quilt top through the center to determine the length. Cut 2 pieced strips to the length measured. Stitch the strips to the quilt sides. Press the seam allowances toward the border strips. Measure the quilt top through the center, including the borders, to determine the width. Cut the remaining 2 pieced strips to the length measured. Stitch the strips to the top and bottom edges of the quilt. Press the seam allowances toward the border strips.

10. Stitch 2 middle border strips together end to end to make one long strip. Make 4. Measure the quilt top through the center to determine the length and width. Cut 2 pieced strips to the length measured. Stitch 2 strips to the quilt sides. Cut 2 pieced strips to the width measured. Stitch the middle border corner posts to each end of the strips. Stitch the strips to the top and bottom edges of the quilt. Press the seam allowances toward the border strips.

11. Measure the quilt top through the center to determine the length. Cut 2 outer border strips to the exact measurement and stitch to the quilt sides. Press the seam allowances toward the border strips.

Measure the quilt top through the center to determine the width. Cut the remaining 2 outer border strips to the exact measurement and stitch the strips to the top and bottom edges of the quilt. Press the seam allowances toward the border strips.

Finishing

Refer to "Fine Finishes" on pages 19–24.

1. Embroider and appliqué any desired block details.
2. Stitch the backing pieces together along the long edges to make 1 piece, 84" x 108"; trim to 74" x 106".
3. Layer the quilt top with batting and backing; baste.
4. Quilt as desired.
5. Square up the quilt top.
6. Add a rod pocket and bind the quilt.
7. Add desired bead or button embellishments.
8. Stitch a label to the quilt back.

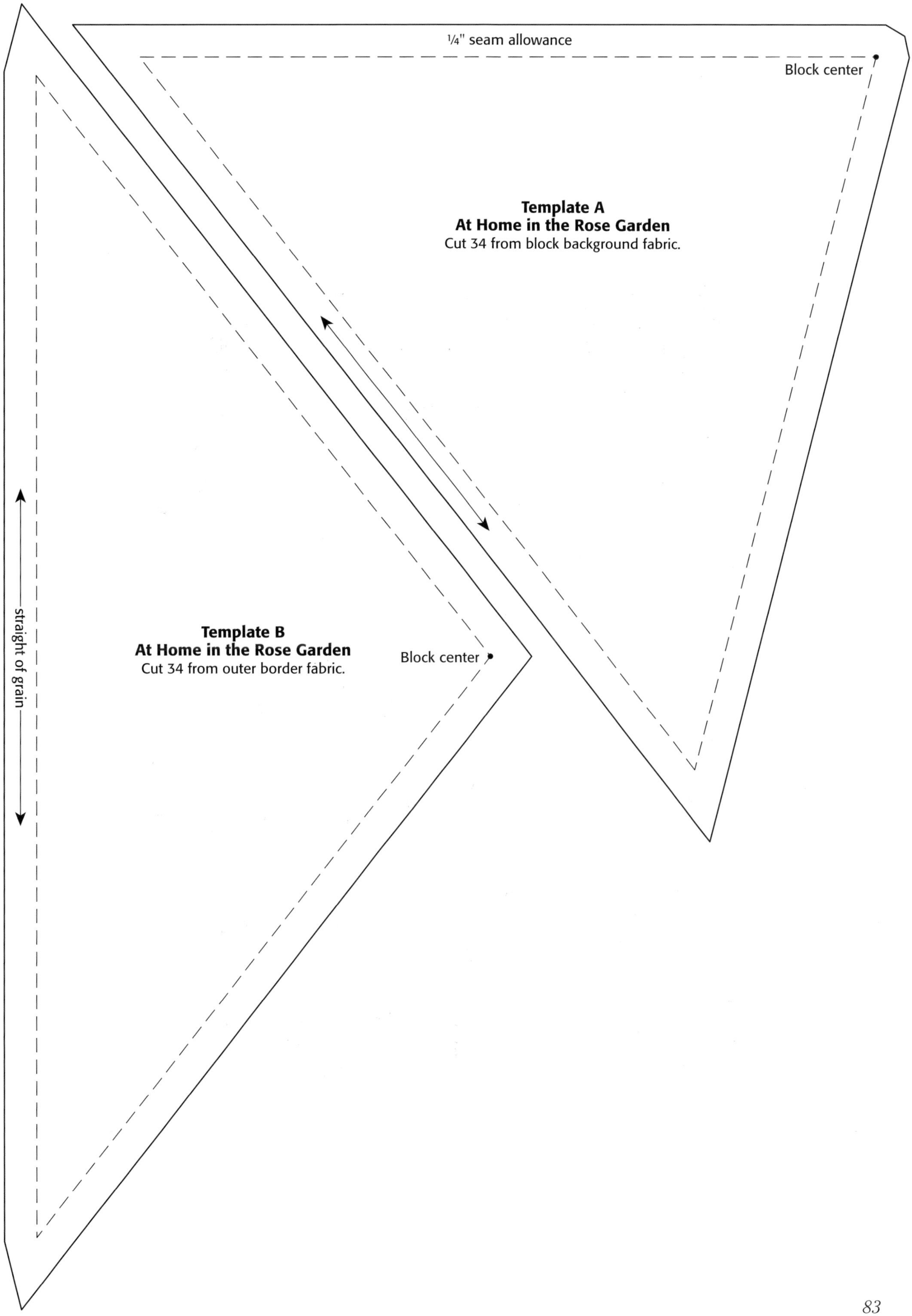

¼" seam allowance

Block center

Template A
At Home in the Rose Garden
Cut 34 from block background fabric.

← straight of grain →

Template B
At Home in the Rose Garden
Cut 34 from outer border fabric.

Block center

Fly Away Home

This quilt was designed to showcase six birdhouses and six bird feeders arranged in a traditional setting. To complement the blocks, bluebird and 4-petal and 5-petal blossom blocks are used as sashing corner posts. What makes this quilt exciting is the dramatic contrast of the overly wide and darkly colored sashing with the bold and brightly colored blocks and corner posts. Create your own bit of drama in your quilt when building these structures. Be bold and dramatic with your fabric and color selections!

Finished size: 53" x 72"

Materials: 42"-wide fabric

2 1/8 yds. for block backgrounds

1/8 yd. each or scraps of 10 to 14 assorted fabrics for birdhouse and feeder structures, leaves, branches, flowers, and bluebirds

1 1/8 yds. for sashing

1/2 yd. for inner border

1/4 yd. for middle border

2 1/2 yds. for outer border and binding

3 3/4 yds. for backing

59" x 78" piece of batting

Assorted buttons and/or appliqué fabrics for entry holes and perches

Cutting

After cutting the following pieces, use the remaining fabrics in the blocks.

From the sashing fabric, cut:

7 strips, each 4 1/2" x 42". Crosscut to make

    15 segments, each 4 1/2" x 7 1/2", for horizontal sashing

    16 segments, each 4 1/2" x 9 1/2", for vertical sashing

From the inner border fabric, cut:

6 strips, each 2" x 42"

From the middle border fabric, cut:

6 strips, each 1" x 42"

From the outer border fabric, cut:

4 strips, each 6 1/2" x 81", along the lengthwise grain for outer borders

4 strips, each 2" x 81", along the lengthwise grain for binding

From the backing fabric, cut:

2 pieces, each 42" x 59"

Assembly

1. Using the 7" x 9" foundation patterns for the birdhouse and bird feeder blocks on pages 25–49, trace 1 each of 6 bird feeder and 6 birdhouse patterns of your choice for a total of 12 blocks.

2. Using the 4" x 4" foundation patterns for the companion blocks on pages 64–68, trace 8 bluebird patterns, reversing 4; five 5-petal blossom patterns; and six 4-petal blossom patterns.

3. Refer to "Steps to Successful Paper Foundation Piecing" (pages 9–15) to construct the blocks, following the Sewing Order and Fabric Keys for each individual block (pages 25–68).

4. Arrange the blocks into 4 horizontal rows of 3 blocks each as shown.

5. To make the block rows, alternately stitch together 4 vertical sashing strips and 3 blocks, beginning and ending with a sashing strip. Make 4. Press the seam allowances toward the sashing strips.

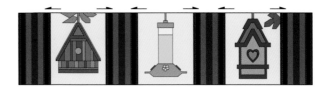

6. To make the sashing rows, alternately stitch together 4 companion blocks and 3 horizontal sashing strips as shown, beginning and ending with the designated companion block. Make 5. Press the seam allowances toward the sashing strips.

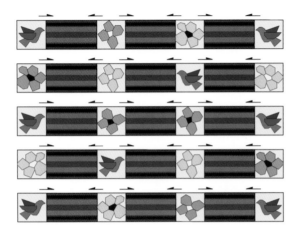

7. Alternating sashing and block rows, stitch the rows together, beginning and ending with a sashing row. Press the seam allowances toward the sashing rows.

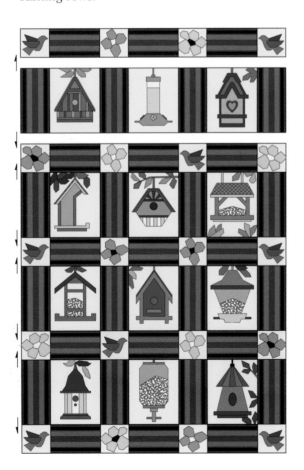

8. To make the side border units, stitch 2 inner border strips together end to end to make one long strip. Make 2. Stitch 2 middle border strips together end to end to make one long strip. Make 2. With center seams matching, stitch together 1 inner border strip and 1 middle border strip along the long edges. Stitch an outer border strip to the middle border strip raw edge. Press the seam allowances toward the outer border. Make 2.

9. To make the top and bottom border units, stitch together 1 inner border strip and 1 middle border strip along the long edges. Stitch an outer border strip to the middle border strip raw edge. Press the seam allowances toward the outer border. Make 2.

10. Measure the quilt top for borders as described in "Making Borders with Mitered Corners" (pages 18–19). Cut the border units to fit and stitch them to the quilt top, mitering the corners.

Finishing

Refer to "Fine Finishes" on pages 19–24.

1. Embroider and appliqué any desired block details.
2. Stitch the backing pieces together along the long edges; trim to 59" x 78".
3. Layer the quilt top with batting and backing; baste.
4. Quilt as desired.
5. Square up the quilt top.
6. Add a rod pocket and bind the quilt.
7. Add desired bead or button embellishments.
8. Stitch a label to the quilt back.

Home for the Holidays

Do you love doves, birdhouses, and Christmas? Here's a wall hanging that ties all three together. Choose a favorite Christmas fabric for the wide outer border, and then build a palette of companion fabrics to use in the blocks and narrower borders and sashing strips. A coordinating stripe is particularly well suited for bringing out holiday sparkle when used as the framing border around each block. Add a Christmas dove to each corner and you're ready to welcome friends and family "home for the holidays."

Finished size: 32$\frac{1}{2}$" x 48"

Materials: 42"-wide fabric

$\frac{3}{4}$ yd. for block backgrounds

$\frac{1}{8}$ yd. each or scraps of 14 to 16 assorted fabrics for birdhouse and feeder structures, leaves, branches, and doves

$\frac{3}{4}$ yd. for sashing and outer border corner block backgrounds

$\frac{3}{8}$ yd. for accent borders

$\frac{3}{8}$ yd. for inner border

$\frac{3}{8}$ yd. for inner border corner posts and binding

$\frac{3}{4}$ yd. for outer border and sashing corner posts

1$\frac{3}{4}$ yds. for backing

38" x 54" piece of batting

Assorted buttons and/or appliqué fabrics for entry holes and perches

4 seed beads for birds' eyes

Cutting

After cutting the following pieces, use the remaining fabrics in the blocks.

From the sashing fabric, cut:

5 strips, 2$\frac{1}{2}$" x 42". Crosscut to make:

    9 strips, each 2$\frac{1}{2}$" x 10", for vertical sashing

    8 strips, each 2$\frac{1}{2}$" x 8", for horizontal sashing

From the accent border fabric, cut:

6 strips, $\frac{3}{4}$" x 42", for block framing border

4 strips, $\frac{3}{4}$" x 42", for quilt accent border

From the inner border fabric, cut:

4 strips, 2" x 42"

From the inner border corner post and binding fabric, cut:

4 strips, each 2" x 42", for binding

1 strip, 2" x 42". Crosscut to make 4 squares, each 2" x 2", for inner border corner posts.

From the outer border fabric, cut:

4 strips, each 4$\frac{1}{2}$" x 42", for outer border

1 strip, 2$\frac{1}{2}$" x 42". Crosscut to make 12 squares, each 2$\frac{1}{2}$" x 2$\frac{1}{2}$", for sashing corner posts.

From the backing fabric, cut:

1 piece, 38" x 54"

Assembly

1. Using the 7" x 9" foundation patterns for the birdhouse blocks on pages 25–49, trace 1 each of any 6 patterns.

2. Using the 4" x 4" foundation patterns for the companion blocks on pages 64–68, trace 4 dove patterns, reversing 2, and 12 blossom patterns.

3. Refer to "Steps to Successful Paper Foundation Piecing" (pages 9–15) to construct the blocks, following the Sewing Order and Fabric Keys for each individual block (pages 25–68).

4. Refer to "Framing Your Projects" (pages 15–18) for directions on applying the accent border strips to each block. Measure each block; each one should be approximately the same size when finished.

5. Arrange the birdhouse blocks in 3 rows of 2 birdhouses each as desired.

6. To make the block rows, alternately stitch together 2 birdhouse blocks and 3 vertical sashing segments, beginning and ending with a sashing segment. Press the seam allowances toward the sashing segments. Make 3.

7. To make the sashing rows, alternately sew together 3 sashing corner posts and 2 horizontal sashing segments, beginning and ending with a corner post. Press the seam allowances toward the sashing segment. Make 4.

8. Alternately sew the sashing rows and the block rows together, beginning and ending with a sash-

ing row. Press the seam allowances toward the sashing rows.

9. Refer to "Framing Your Projects" (pages 15–18) for directions on applying the accent border strips to the quilt top.

10. Measure the quilt top through the center to determine its length and width. Cut 2 inner border strips the quilt length measurement for the sides; cut 2 inner border strips the quilt width measurement for the top and bottom edges. Stitch the side borders to the quilt sides. Press the seam allowances toward the border strips. Stitch the inner border corner posts to each end of the top and bottom strips. Stitch the pieced strips to the quilt top and bottom edges. Press the seam allowances toward the border strips.

11. Measure the quilt top through the center to determine its length and width. Cut 2 outer border strips the quilt length measurement for the sides; cut 2 outer border strips the quilt width measurement for the top and bottom edges. Stitch the side borders to the quilt sides. Press the seam allowances toward the border strips. Stitch a Dove block to each end of the top and bottom strips, making sure the doves are facing each other. Stitch the pieced strips to the quilt top and bottom edges. Press the seam allowances toward the border strips.

Finishing

Refer to "Fine Finishes" on pages 19–24.

1. Embroider and appliqué any desired block details.
2. Layer the quilt top with batting and backing; baste.
3. Quilt as desired.
4. Square up the quilt top.
5. Add a rod pocket and bind the quilt.
6. Add any desired bead or button embellishments.
7. Stitch a label to the quilt back.

It's a Birds' Picnic in the Park

Let a bright floral print prompt your other fabric choices as you construct all six of the 7" x 9" bird feeders and line them up in this vertical arrangement.

Finished size: 22" x 79"

Materials: 42"-wide fabric

7/8 yd. for bird feeder block and bird block backgrounds

1/8 yd. each or scraps of 14 to18 assorted fabrics for birdhouse and feeder structures, leaves, branches, and birds

1/2 yd. for sashing and inner border corner posts

3/8 yd. for sashing corner posts and outer accent border

1/4 yd. for inner accent border

3/8 yd. for inner border

2 7/8 yds. for outer border and backing

28" x 85" piece of batting

3/8 yd. for binding

4 seed beads for birds' eyes

Cutting

After cutting the following pieces, use the remaining fabrics in the blocks.

From the sashing and inner border corner post fabric, cut:

5 strips, each 2 1/2" x 42". Crosscut to make:

    7 strips, each 2 1/2" x 7 1/2", for horizontal sashing

    12 strips, each 2 1/2" x 9 1/2", for vertical sashing

    4 squares, each 1 1/2" x 1 1/2", for inner border corner posts

From the sashing corner posts and outer accent border fabric, cut:

5 strips, each 3/4" x 42", for outer accent border

1 strip, 2 1/2" x 42". Crosscut to make 12 squares, each 2 1/2" x 2 1/2", for sashing corner posts.

From the inner accent border fabric, cut:

5 strips, each 3/4" x 42"

From the inner border fabric, cut:

5 strips, each 1½" x 42"

From the outer border and backing fabric, cut:

2 strips, each 4½" x 90", along the lengthwise grain. Crosscut to make:

    2 strips, each 4½" x 71½", for the outer side borders

    2 strips, each 4½" x 14½", for the outer top and bottom borders

1 piece, 28" x 85", for backing

From the binding fabric, cut:

5 strips, each 2" x 42"

Assembly

1. Using the 7" x 9" foundation patterns for the bird feeder blocks on pages 25–49, trace 1 each of the 6 patterns.

2. Using the 4" x 4" foundation patterns for the Chickadee block on page 67, trace 4 patterns, reversing 2.

3. Refer to "Steps to Successful Paper Foundation Piecing" (pages 9–15) to construct the blocks, following the Sewing Order and Fabric Keys for each individual block (pages 25–67).

4. Arrange the 6 bird feeder blocks vertically as desired. Stitch a vertical sashing strip to the sides of each block. Press the seam allowances toward the sashing strips.

5. To make the sashing rows, stitch together 2 sashing corner posts and 1 horizontal sashing strip, beginning and ending with a corner post. Press the seam allowances toward the sashing strip. Make 7.

6. Alternately sew the sashing rows and block rows together, beginning and ending with a sashing row. Press the seam allowances toward the sashing rows.

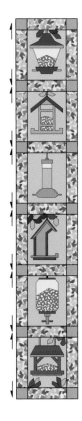

7. Stitch 2 inner accent border strips together end to end to make one long strip. Make 2. Refer to "Framing Your Projects" (pages 15–18) for directions on applying the pieced accent border strips to the quilt sides. Use the remaining inner accent border strip for the quilt top and bottom edges.

8. Measure the quilt top through the center to determine its length and width. Stitch 2 inner border strips together end to end to make one long strip. Make 2. Cut each strip to the length measured. Refer to "Framing Your Projects" (pages 15–18) to stitch the strips to the quilt sides. Press the seam allowances toward the border strips. From the remaining inner border strip, cut 2 strips the width

measured. Stitch an inner border corner post to the ends of each strip. Stitch the strips to the quilt top and bottom edges. Press the seam allowances toward the border strips.

outer border corner posts to the ends of each top and bottom strip, making sure the chickadees are facing each other. Stitch the strips to the quilt top and bottom edges. Press the seam allowances toward the border strips.

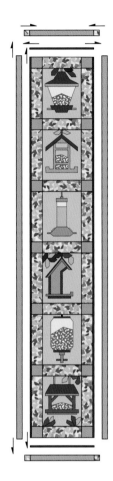

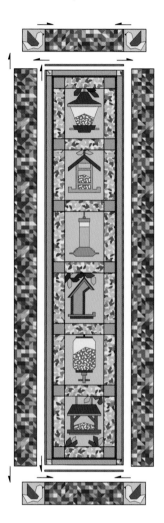

9. Stitch 2 outer accent border strips together end to end to make one long strip. Make 2. Refer to "Framing Your Projects" (pages 15–18) for directions on applying the pieced accent border strips to the quilt sides. Use the remaining outer accent border strip for the quilt top and bottom edges.

10. Measure the quilt top through the center to determine its length and width. Cut 2 outer side border strips the length measured; cut 2 outer top and bottom strips the width measured. Refer to "Framing Your Projects" (pages 15–18) to stitch the side borders to the quilt sides. Press the seam allowances toward the border strips. Stitch the

Finishing

Refer to "Fine Finishes" on pages 19–24.

1. Embroider and appliqué any desired block details.
2. Layer the quilt top with batting and backing; baste.
3. Quilt as desired.
4. Square up the quilt top.
5. Add a rod pocket and bind the quilt.
6. Add any desired bead or button embellishments.
7. Stitch a label to the quilt back.

Springtime Delight

Whether it's spring, summer, fall, or winter, let your quilt reflect your favorite season. Spring is the season highlighted here. The branches are just now filling out with fresh green leaves, and the raspberry-colored buttons are serving as the abundant blossoms.

Choose any four of the 7" x 9" blocks, arrange them horizontally, and surround them with an all-over leaf print. Place some birds in the corners, and you must agree that it is delightful when it's spring!

Finished size: 47" x 35"

Materials: 42"-wide fabric

⅞ yd. for birdhouse block background

1 yd. for branch block background

⅛ yd. *each* or scraps of 10 to 14 assorted fabrics for birdhouse blocks

¼ yd. *each* or scraps of 4 assorted green fabrics for leaves

½ yd. for branch and outer border unit

⅝ yd. for sashing and inner border

¼ yd. for accent border

1⅛ yds. for outer border unit inner and outer strips and binding

1 fat quarter of bird print for outer border corner posts

1⅝ yds. for backing

54" x 40" piece of batting

Green embroidery floss

Assorted buttons and/or appliqué fabrics for berries, entry holes, and perches

Cutting

After cutting the following pieces, use the remaining fabrics in the blocks.

From the branch and outer border center strip fabric, cut:

4 strips, each 1¼" x 42", for outer border unit

From the sashing and inner border fabric, cut:

7 strips, each 2½" x 42". Crosscut to make:

    3 strips, each 2½" x 9½", for vertical sashing

    4 strips, each 2½" x 34½", for horizontal sashing

    2 strips, each 2½" x 26½", for inner side borders

From the accent border fabric, cut:

4 strips, each 1" x 42"

From the outer border fabric, cut:

8 strips, each 2⅛" x 42", for outer border unit

4 strips, each 2" x 42", for binding

From the bird print fabric, cut:

4 squares, each 4½" x 4½", with a bird centered in the square for outer border corner posts

Assembly

1. Using the 7" x 9" foundation patterns for the birdhouse blocks on pages 25–49, trace 1 each of any 4 birdhouse patterns of your choice.

2. Using the 17½" x 4½" foundation pattern for the branch on pages 69–71, trace 4 complete patterns, reversing 2.

3. Refer to "Steps to Successful Paper Foundation Piecing" (pages 9–15) to construct the blocks, following the Sewing Order and Fabric Keys for each individual block (pages 25–69).

4. To make the branch sections, stitch together 1 regular and 1 reversed branch block end to end as shown to make one long block. Make 2.

5. Arrange the 4 birdhouse blocks in 1 horizontal row as desired. Stitch a vertical sashing strip between each block. Press the seam allowances toward the sashing strips.

6. Stitch a horizontal sashing strip to the top and bottom of the block unit. Stitch a branch unit to the quilt top and bottom edges so the branch is curved toward the block unit. Stitch the remaining horizontal sashing strips to the quilt top and bottom edges. Press the seam allowances toward the sashing strips. Stitch the inner side borders to the quilt sides. Press the seam allowances toward the border strips.

(pages 15–18) to stitch the side borders to the quilt sides. Press the seam allowances toward the border strips. Stitch the outer border corner posts to the ends of each top and bottom strip, making sure the birds are facing the desired direction. Stitch the strips to the quilt top and bottom edges. Press the seam allowances toward the border strips.

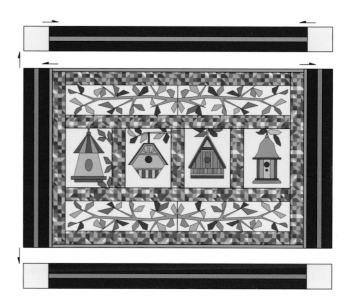

7. Refer to "Framing Your Project" (pages 15–18) to stitch the accent borders to the quilt top and bottom edges, then the sides.

8. To make the outer border unit, stitch a $2^1/8$" x 42" outer border strip to each side of a $1^1/4$" x 42" outer border center strip. Make 4.

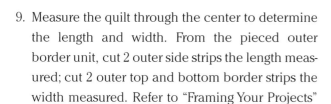

9. Measure the quilt through the center to determine the length and width. From the pieced outer border unit, cut 2 outer side strips the length measured; cut 2 outer top and bottom border strips the width measured. Refer to "Framing Your Projects"

Finishing

Refer to "Fine Finishes" on pages 19–24.

1. Using 2 strands of green floss, stem stitch (page 20) the outer edges of the light colored leaves. Embroider or appliqué any other desired block details.
2. Layer the quilt top with batting and backing; baste.
3. Quilt as desired.
4. Square up the quilt top.
5. Add a rod pocket and bind the quilt.
6. Add desired bead or button embellishments.
7. Stitch a label to the quilt back.

About the Author

Jaynette Huff's interest in quilting began more than thirty years ago when a group of women offered to share their quilting knowledge and skills with her. She has been quilting ever since.

Jaynette's first career was teaching high school English and speech. After completing her master's degree in business administration (M.B.A.) and her coursework for her Ph.D. in management, she spent the next twelve years teaching at the college level. It was teaching "Small Business Management" that lead to the next career move—owning and operating her own quilt shop.

Her professional quilting life began in August of 1992 when she opened the quilt shop, Idle-Hour Quilts and Design, in Conway, Arkansas. For the next eight and a half years she was kept very busy running this business. In 2000, Jaynette's book *Needles and Notions* was published by Martingale & Company.

Desiring more time to work on her own projects, Jaynette now works full time at home, writing, designing, and quilting! Her quilts have won several awards and have appeared in numerous quilt magazines and books.

Jaynette Huff lives in Conway with her husband, Larry, their cat, Inky, and Buddy, a miniature schnauzer.